8837

New Hope for the Nineties

THE COMING GREAT AWAKENING

David L. McKenna

INTERVARSITY PRESS
DOWNERS GROVE, ILLINOIS 60515

InterVarsity Press is the book-publishing division of InterVarsity Christian Fellowship, a student movement active on campus at hundreds of universities, colleges and schools of nursing in the United States of America, and a member movement of the International Fellowship of Evangelical Students. For information about local and regional activities, write Public Relations Dept., InterVarsity Christian Fellowship, 6400 Schroeder Rd., P.O. Box 7895, Madison, WI 53707-7895.

All Scripture quotations, unless otherwise indicated, are from the Holy Bible, New International Version. Copyright © 1973, 1978, International Bible Society. Used by permission of Zondervan Bible Publishers.

Cover illustration: Rob Ebersol

ISBN 0-8308-1735-2

Printed in the United States of America ∞

Library of Congress Cataloging-in-Publication Data

McKenna, David L. (David Loren), 1929-
    The coming great awakening: new hope for the nineties/by David
McKenna.
        p.   cm.
    Includes bibliographical references.
    ISBN 0-8308-1735-2
    1. College students—Religious life.   2. Revivals—United States-
-History.   3. Church renewal.   I. Title.
BV4531.2.M295   1990
269—dc20   90-48722
                                                                              CIP

---

13   12   11   10   9   8   7   6   5   4   3   2   1
99   98   97   96   95   94   93   92   91   90

Introduction

I am a realistic optimist. Simply put, I do not believe that God has given up on our world.

The basis for my perspective comes from a well-known Bible story. In the book of 1 Kings the prophet Elijah is introduced to us. His wins and losses, ups and downs, unfold like the saga of our own lives. After he triumphed over the priests of Baal on Mount Carmel when heaven-sent fire consumed his sacrifice, Elijah goes into an emotional slump. He fears for his life, complains about his calling and feels all alone as the prophet of God. His depressed state drives him under a broom tree to moan and into a cave to die. While he is in the cave, the "word of the Lord" comes to him with the question "What are you doing here, Elijah?" (19:9).

Elijah voices his complaint once again, "I am the only one left, and now they are trying to kill me too."

God responds to this scared cave-dweller, "Go out and stand on the mount before the LORD." Then comes the clincher *"and behold, the LORD passed by"* (19:11 KJV). From the perspective of the mountaintop, Elijah sees that God is still at work in the world, hears the word that he will not die and receives the assurance that there are seven thousand people in Israel who have not betrayed their Lord.

Now you know why I am an optimist. In a cave we have no perspective at all. Plato, in his famous Allegory of the Cave, tells us that cave-dwellers mistake the shadows on the wall for the reality of life. But out of the cave and up on the mountaintop, we gain perspective. From the vista of an elevated view, we look and exclaim with awe, "Behold, the Lord is passing by!" Then we know that God has not given up on our world, that our life is not futile and that we are not alone. From the perspective of the mountaintop, we can see the signs of a great spiritual awakening in our generation. Not that we close our eyes to the reality of human sin, moral decline and social chaos. But when we look through the eyes of faith from a lofty height, we cannot deny *the promise of God:* "In the last days, God says, I will pour out my Spirit on all people. Your sons and daughters will prophesy, your young men [and women] will see visions, your old men [and women] will dream dreams" (Acts 2:17).

The Perspective of the Past
Furthermore, from the *perspective of history* we can see that this promise of Pentecost has been fulfilled time and time again. Especially in American history, at the end of each century, the signs of spiritual awakening have been evident. In the 1790s and the 1890s, the record is most clear. The Spirit of God visited Christian students on college campuses with an outpouring of his Spirit and gave them visions for renewing our churches, reforming our culture and redeeming our world. These were called Great Awakenings.

What about the 1990s? Is God's promise still good? Will history repeat itself? Here is where our book begins. When we glance quickly at the decades since World War 2, we can see the signs of the Lord preparing us for another Great Awakening (chapter 1—"Stirrings of the Spirit"). These signs are even more pronounced when we view the happenings among Christian students on college campuses in the 1790s and 1890s. Stirrings of the Spirit in those decades brought earlier mid-century awakenings to fulfillment and also set the stage for a Great Awakening to come (chapter 2—"Heirs of a Haystack").

Naturally, our curiosity causes us to ask the question "Is there a pattern of awakenings in past centuries which helps us see where we are now?" The answer is yes. There is a rising-and-falling pattern in the history of Great Awakenings that scholars have discovered. In this pattern we can see where we are now in the 1990s and take hope (chapter 3—"The Cycle of the Spirit").

The Perspective of the Present
Like Robert Benchley's "killey-doo bird," we have taken off backward in our book to see where we have been in the history of Great Awakenings in America. Then we can turn and look forward to see where we are going. If God chooses to pour out his Spirit on all people once again in the 1990s, the college campus is still the tender spot where cultural conflict is most intense (chapter 4—"The Campus: Center of Stress").

College students bear the brunt of cultural conflict because of their vulnerability to stress and their sensitivity to moral and spiritual matters (chapter 5—"The Student: Candidate for Conversion"). If the pattern of the past holds, college students in the 1990s who come to Christ will find each other and form small groups for personal support and spiritual nurture (chapter 6—"The Cell: School for Spirituality"). And, if history repeats itself, the students will not let the cell groups turn inwardly and become self-serving. Rather, they will find the natural connections among Christian students through which the Spirit of God will move from campus to campus and from continent to continent until the globe is covered (chapter 7—"The Network: Instrument for Evangelism").

Who will lead a Great Awakening in the 1990s? This question is crucial in a time when the credibility of legitimate leaders is so low. But again, in the "cycle of the Spirit," God raises up visionary leaders with prophetic voices just as he promised in his word (chapter 8—"The Leader: Agent of Hope"). The American church awaits the vision and voice of prophetic leaders who will show the way through the moral jungle of our time; the church awaits the outpouring of God's Spirit in the final decade of the twentieth century (chapter 9—"The Church: Body for Renewal"). The culture also groans for deliverance from the forces of decay which threaten our future. Only a Great Awakening can make the difference in rebuilding the moral base on which our freedom rests (chapter 10—"The Culture: Field for Reform"). Revival among the masses, renewal in the church, and reform in the culture is the full cycle of a Great Awakening.

The Perspective for the Future

Is another Great Awakening on the way as we come to the close of the twentieth century? The answer is yes. We have the *pattern* of American history, the *perspective* of global revival, and the *promise* of God's Word. As these facts converge with the open mind and ready spirit of Christian students on college campuses in the 1990s, we can foresee another Great Awakening (chapter 11—"Anticipating the Great Awakening"). For now, we must watch and wait: watch the stirring of God's Spirit and wait for the outpouring when the young see visions. In those visions we see our hope.

My thanks go to the students whose thirst for God prompted me to write this book. I especially thank my son Rob, a graduate of Seattle Pacific University in the class of 1990, who represents so well the mind and heart of today's college student. When he reflected on the church, he concluded, "The passion is missing"; when he thought about the campus, he said, "We need a revival," and when he planned his own career, he testified, "Whatever I do must be ministry." In simple sentences without fluff or flair, Rob spoke more truth than most of us can write in volumes. His vision tells me that the Spirit of God is upon him, and his passion tells me that he is ready and willing to participate in the coming Great Awakening.

Thanks also to Sheila Lovell, my executive assistant, for editing the book, researching the endnotes and finishing the final draft when we were shorthanded in the office. Credit for work on the preliminary draft goes to Lois Mulcahy, former secretary to the president, who deferred her move to a better position in Washington, D.C., until she completed the copy.

Though I have written with college students in my mind's eye, anyone who is ready to "hear what the Spirit says to the churches" through its young people will identify with the book. In fact, may all who read be rewarded with the vision of the young.

David L. McKenna

Prolog

Memo to a College Student

What motivates an author to write? The stimulus may be as sublime as the apostle Paul's when he exhorted the Corinthians, "What I am writing to you is the Lord's command" (1 Cor 14:37). Or it may be as laughable as Ernest Hemingway's response to a reporter who asked what was the greatest inspiration for his writing. Hemingway answered, "The publisher's deadline."

A mix of motives prompted me to write this book. Because college students always want to "get under the skin" of the person who teaches them or learns with them, my first task is to bring you into the motive for my writing.

A Prayer of Passion

How do you put a prayer into print without losing its passion? Usually when we think about books for college students, we expect an orderly, well-written exposition of ideas, facts and values. How well I remember my thesis for the master's degree in counseling psychology. I did an inductive and integrated Bible study on the personality and practice of Jesus as a psychological counselor. After reviewing the first draft of the thesis, my advisor told me, "Get yourself out of it." He wanted me to take my personality out of the material. So I went about the clinical task of objectifying the study in order to give it research credibility. After I received my degree the same faculty advisor encouraged me to prepare the manuscript for publication under the title *The Jesus Model.* Irony of ironies, the publisher who reviewed the manuscript wrote back, "Put yourself into it!"

Without apology, then, I have written this book with "me" in it. While it is not even close to the artistic level of Michelangelo, I know a bit about his passion for work when he saw an angel in a block of marble waiting to be released. Compulsion as much as inspiration has motivated me to write. Every word is a release of passion driven by prayer. If I had only one book to write, this would be it!

A Sense of Urgency

My passion is matched by urgency. In one sense the 1990s will be just another decade against the timelessness of eternity. But the opposite is also true. The decade of the 1990s not only closes a century, it opens a millennium. Whether by divine prompting or human impulse, there is an air of spiritual expectancy for the 1990s that cannot be denied.

Because I grew up in a climate of end-time predictions, I am repulsed by claims of direct revelation or tendencies toward ecstatic overstatement in order to draw attention and sell books. Yet, as I have the opportunity to interact with the broad spectrum of theological thought and Christian ministries today, one indisputable fact stands out: *There are stirrings of the Spirit in all sectors of the globe, which are converging with earth-shaking force.*

Especially among the young is the converging of the Spirit unmistakable. Again, I would be the first to resist any attempt to harness these forces by artificial means or to accelerate them by human effort. But just as quickly, I would be the first to risk myself—either to move with the mysterious winds of the Spirit or to get out of his way—in order to see another great spiritual awakening in our generation.

A Tract for Our Times

My prayer of passion and my sense of urgency are not just rockets sent up to burst over college and university campuses with a spectacular show of wisdom and foresight. Everything I write is conditioned by my profound respect for the mind and heart of the college student. I know, for instance, that you have a "nose for the genuine." Anyone who plays spiritual games with you is summarily dismissed. I know too that your passion exceeds mine. We both have the burning desire for spiritual awakening, but you have the boundless energy to bring it off and see it through. Nor can I forget that your impatience exceeds my urgency. When Paul urged Timothy to "fan into flame the gift of God, which is in you through the laying on of my hands" (2 Tim 1:6), he recognized the youthful passion that energizes your gift to get the right things done.

So, as I thought about your expectations for this book, one thought dominated my mind: *Make it a fast-moving, hard-hitting field manual for college students who wait on edge for a spiritual awakening in our generation.* Without apology, then, the book is brief, the chapters are short, the words are crisp, and the ideas are progressively highlighted in italics.

Like the poet who said, "A poem is never finished; it is abandoned in despair," I, too, feel as if the book is incomplete. My prayer is that the synergy of the Spirit will fuse my urgency with your vision as we await for the exponential power of Pentecost. If so, in the coming Great Awakening, you will write the last chapter.

With his promise,

David L. McKenna

1 | *Stirrings of the Spirit*

Are you ready for a great spiritual awakening? Even now, you can see the stirrings of the Spirit across the face of the earth. In the oppressed nations they are blowing with gale force as winds of freedom. In the Two-Thirds World they are moving with the transforming power of the mighty, rushing winds of Pentecost. But what about the West, especially in North America? Has God given up on our society or passed us by? Are the evangelical prophets of doom, who squint into the twilight and fix their eyes on the darkness, right about our civilization?

I say no. God has not given up on us. If we watch closely we can see the stirrings of the Spirit among us today. Perhaps it is only as perceptible as a rustle in the mulberry bush. Yet the mysterious movement cannot be denied. In fact, secular prophets such as John Naisbitt in *Megatrends 2000* already foresee spiritual revival in America as we anticipate a third millennium.[1]

For those of us who see through the eyes of faith, the stirrings are clearer still. As I said in the introduction, we live each day with the promise of God in Acts 2:17, which has been fulfilled time and time again. Since the founding of America our history has been written in cycles of spiritual renewal that can be attributed only to the Spirit of God. Especially in the 1790s and 1890s, history records stirrings of the Spirit among college students, who have not only brought a spiritual awakening to full cycle in each century but also set the spiritual tone and the moral agenda for the century to come. So if history repeats itself in the 1990s, another Great Awakening is already on the way. *When did it begin? How has it developed? Where are we now?* And most important, *will it begin again among Christian students on the college campus?*

To answer these questions we need to see how the stirrings of the Spirit since World War 2 have been preparing us for the coming Great Awakening of the 1990s.

The Fabulous Fifties: Steady State
After expending high energy on World War 2, Americans settled back into a decade which sociologist Anthony F. C. Wallace would describe as a "steady state"—a time when the moral consensus is strong, established institutions such as the home, the church and the school are stable, and legitimate leaders are accepted with confidence.[2] President Dwight D. Eisenhower symbolized the optimism of those days with his contagious smile and his "V" for victory hand signal.

Except for Senator McCarthy's "witch hunts" against Communists and Eisenhower's warning against the growing military-industrial complex, Americans looked positively toward the reconstruction of postwar society by refocusing the American dream with higher education as the dream-maker. The vision of equal opportunity in education included a tuition-free community college within commuting distance for every American at the base of a system that rose to its peak in the prestige of national research universities, such as Michigan and Berkeley. Education, in effect, became the religion of postwar America, with its theology of equal opportunity, its sanctuary of the campus, its salvation in science, its communion in group dynamics and its nurture in counseling and student development.

Yet the minds of students were as "quiet as mice." Except for occasional forays into existentialist philosophy—championed by Jean-Paul Sartre's conclusion that "man is a useless passion"[3]—their self-satisfaction matched the mood of the nation.

Predictions of Things to Come

Two events, one at the beginning of the decade and one at the end, served as predictors for things to come. *In 1950, a spirit of revival revitalized the Christian college campus.* Following the precedent of earlier revivals on campus, small bands of students met for prayer on such campuses as Asbury, Wheaton and Seattle Pacific. Then the unexplainable happened. From their prayer cells, the students carried their testimonies of personal confession into chapel services and caught a deepening sense of conviction for sin among the students. Some of the chapel services continued for hours and days, always in order and unmistakably solemnized by holy awe.

Out of these revivals came the leaders for evangelical Christianity for the next forty years or more. In one way or another, Billy Graham, Carl F. H. Henry, Harold Ockenga, Robert Cook, Bill Bright and many other prominent evangelical leaders are linked to these life-changing moments. Out of these revivals, a new phase of the parachurch movement also came into being. With a special emphasis on young people in educational settings, Youth for Christ, Young Life, Campus Crusade, Navigators and InterVarsity Christian Fellowship were either born or reborn for ministry in the decade ahead.

Toward the end of the decade, a second prophetic event took place. *The Soviet Sputnik satellite beat every American contender into space.* Momentarily, at least, the intoxicating influence of our scientific superiority, which had given us the secular promise of being humankind's "chosen people," received a sobering jolt. The Soviets, our allies during World War 2, now became our competitors for world superiority through nuclear arms. And this contest only now, three decades later, has hope of ending.

Not even these prophetic events, however, could shake our "steady state" society in the 1950s. Our economy boomed, government grew, education flourished, television entertained and mainline churches reaped the benefits of cultural and civil Christianity in church attendance and new members.

The Sobering Sixties: A World Turned Upside-Down

The 1960s opened with the lofty vision that the decade would be the "Soaring Sixties." John F. Kennedy's election as president not only broke down the prejudice against a Roman Catholic in the White House, but his boyish face, his visionary outlook and his memorable eloquence brought with it the promise of Camelot. Who can ever forget Kennedy's inaugural call, "Ask not what your country can do for you, but ask what you can do for your country"? Or whose spine does not tingle to recall his goals, "To put a man on the moon and end hunger in America before the end of the decade"? Only comedians with a cynical bent spoofed the reign of Jack and Bobby Kennedy as "the grim world of the brothers wonderful."

Then it happened! The world turned upside-down with the staccato beat of revolutionary events that can best be remembered by the places where they happened:

Dallas (1963)—the assassination of John Kennedy

Selma (1965)—the beating of Blacks and others marching for civil rights

Detroit (1967)—the race riot that charred a city

Memphis (1968)—the assassination of Martin Luther King

Chicago (1968)—the disruption of the Democratic National Convention

Los Angeles (1968)—the assassination of Robert Kennedy

Berkeley (1969)—the beginning of the campus revolt

Woodstock (1969)—the glorification of illegal drugs, free sex and rock music

My Lai (1969)—the massacre of innocent Vietnamese villagers by U.S. troops

Kent State (1970)—the shooting of student protesters by the National Guard

Not since the time when secession threatened the Union in the 1860s had Americans been in greater conflict. Every moral value undergirding the social consensus came into question; every mediating institution—home, church, school, business and government—teetered on crumbling foundations; and every legitimate leader suffered a loss of credibility.

The intensity of the conflict centered on the college campus. Minds that had been as "quiet as mice" now turned so bitter that on the cue of Jerry Rubin's cry "Do it," students responded with protests, boycotts, trashings and even bombings. Like ghetto-dwellers who burn down their own homes in frustrated protest against an unjust system, students took out their rage on trustees, administrators and professors who symbolized the Establishment that they felt had betrayed them.

In one class at Harvard, for example, the students demanded pass-fail grades when they boycotted classes and marched in protest during the final days of the spring semester. The professor succumbed to their demands. The next year, however, one of the students came back and demanded a letter grade in order to qualify for admission to graduate school. When the professor pointed out the contradictory demand, the student answered, "Just because we panicked, we didn't expect *you* to!" The student's barbed point illustrates how close we came to total cultural breakdown during those troublesome days. Our moral mazeways of the past dead-ended, our established institutions foundered and our traditional leaders panicked. Psychiatrists who observed the conflict reported that *our circle of sanity was badly bent, if not almost broken.*

The Surprising Seventies: One Divine Moment

In the midst of the cultural revolution of the 1960s and early 1970s, Americans became a "stressed-out" people. Rather than turning to religion for help, however, we entered an era of "therapeutic theology" based on an odd mixture of psychoanalytical theory, Eastern mysticism and group dynamics, with a dash of evangelical fervor. A multimillion-dollar market developed overnight with exotic programs such as Esalen, popular movements such as Transactional Analysis, and spin-offs such as motivational seminars, stress-reduction workshops and human-potential clinics.

A standing joke of the time defined a neurotic as a person who built air castles, a psychotic as a person who lived in them, and a psychiatrist as the one who collected the rent. To symbolize the era, a best-selling book of the late 1960s captured the American mind and popularized Transactional Analysis under the reassuring title *I'm O.K., You're O.K.* by Thomas A. Harris.[4]

Evangelical Christians revealed their own individual stress of the era by extolling *I'm O.K., You're O.K.* as a spiritual discovery and then added their own version of relational theology in Keith Miller's evangelical best seller *A Taste of New Wine.*[5] Relational theology, from Keith Miller's book to Robert Schuller's television sermons, took off with spectacular success as stress-reduction systems with spiritual overtones. No one disputes relational theology according to its foundational premise, "To affirm in others what Christ affirms in us." Its fault line, however, is exposed when the reality of human sin is downplayed and the resources of human psychology are elevated almost to a redemptive level.

Not all of the responses to individual stress of the 1960s remained at the psychological level. While the media featured students venting their stress by "turning on" to drugs, "turning off" the Establishment and "dropping out" of the system, conviction again settled on the students of such Christian colleges as Asbury, Wheaton, Seattle Pacific, Greenville, Taylor, Houghton, Messiah, Westmont and scores of other schools. In 1970 Asbury College, a school founded in the name of the camp-meeting evangelist and circuit-rider of American Methodism, experienced another revival on campus. A chapel service ran continuously for five or more days and even made believers out of the skeptical reporters who came to cover the event. *One Divine Moment,* the book that reads like the journal of a campus Pentecost, vibrates with the supernatural.[6]

Although always orderly, the confession, repentance, forgiveness, restitution and sanctification of students reflected the unmistakable evidence of the outpouring of God's Spirit on the campus. Then, following in the footsteps of students in earlier awakenings, Asburians traveled far and wide with the message of revival. But wherever they went, the Spirit of God had preceded them. At Seattle Pacific University, for example, the same sense of holy awe greeted the students coming to chapel and time stood still as the services continued through the night and into the following day. Any doubt about the genuine nature of revival vanished when the "resident radical," who had conspired with public university students to threaten violence on the campus, confessed his sin, asked forgiveness and gave a miraculous testimony to his counterculture friends.

Individual stress also took on the meaning of national spiritual conviction after President Richard Nixon betrayed his oath of office by lying about Watergate. Even though we exiled him to San Clemente as the scapegoat for our sins, most of us discovered the depravity of Watergate within ourselves. From prominent pulpits and syndicated editorials, a national consciousness of sin and need for confession gripped our people. Again, future historians of Great Awakenings will have to account for a Proclamation for a National Day of Humiliation, Fasting and Prayer on April 30, 1974, which Senator Mark Hatfield presented for Senate action. Paralleling a similar proclamation by Abraham Lincoln for April 30, 1863, the text was based on 2 Chronicles 7:14: "If my people, who are called by my name, will humble themselves and pray and seek my face and turn from their wicked ways, then will I hear from heaven and will forgive their sin and will heal their land."

Whether by courtesy or conviction, the Senate passed the resolution by voice vote, but the House never officially took action. While the national press largely ignored its meaning, God did not. *National conviction for human sin prepared the way for national repentance and spiritual revival.*

Mass Conversion: The Born-Again Movement

In 1969 Herman Kahn and Anthony J. Weiner popularized the science of futurism in a book entitled *The Year 2000*.[7] Derived from their laudable success in predicting the needs and proposing the strategies for nuclear warfare, Kahn and Weiner applied their sophisticated techniques to forecasting our social, economic, political, military and religious future. One technique involved projecting current trends on a *straight line* into A.D. 2000 (e.g., population growth). A second technique anticipated *jumps* along the straight line which would speed up programs if certain breakthroughs took place (e.g., medical advancement through laser technology). And still a third technique made provision for *serendipities*, or pleasant surprises, which would literally create a new trend at a higher level (for example, a nuclear arms agreement between the superpowers).

Yet their scientific predictions, backed by experience and intuition, failed to anticipate one of the most sweeping events of the 1970s— the born-again movement. George Gallup, Jr., surprised the nation in 1976 with a poll that showed 45-50 million Americans who professed to be "born-again, Bible-believing and witnessing" Christians. Whether the poll represented the discovery of an existing mass of born-again Americans or the results of a revival among the masses is incidental to the fact that a spiritual movement was on the way: *Time* magazine declared 1976 as The Year of the Evangelical; televangelists vaulted into national prominence; evangelical books accounted for one-third of the publishing market; celebrities in athletics and entertainment openly spoke their faith; and a surprising popular vote elected Jimmy Carter, a born-again Christian, to the presidency.

College students followed suit. Campuses that had been hotbeds of violent protest a few years earlier now openly accepted the gospel as a viable belief. No student had to apologize for being a born-again Christian.

Evangelical Christian colleges fared even better. At the close of the 1960s they were predicted to go bankrupt by 1976 because they could not compete with the convenient, comprehensive and economical public institutions. As to their impact on society, a 1970 Carnegie Commission study labeled them "invisible colleges."[8] But the reports failed to take into consideration the 1970 campus revival and the 1976 born-again movement. Instead of going bankrupt or disappearing, they banded together in a Christian College Consortium to develop their distinctive mission for integrating faith and learning. Ably handling their limited resources, these colleges attracted growing numbers of students to the "redemptive community" of their campus. To their credit, Christian colleges served as a source for revitalizing evangelical Christianity through the campus revival of 1970 and then rode the high tide of the born-again movement in 1976 by responding to the intellectual, social and spiritual growth needs of its regenerated youth.

The Enigmatic Eighties: The Moral Majority and Others
In the spiritual pattern that leads to a Great Awakening, we can expect prophetic voices that proclaim the gospel with relevance to changing needs. Whether we agree with his theology or his tactics, we cannot deny that the most visible and vocal spokesperson following the born-again movement was the Rev. Jerry Falwell. His creation of the Moral Majority has to be recognized as a stroke of genius. Under standing how the mass media breaks down institutional loyalties but builds networks of special interest, Falwell put together a collection of co-belligerents—fundamentalist Christians, Roman Catholics, Jews, Mormons and anyone else who concurred with his pro-life, pro-family, pro-decency and pro-American agenda. Ironically, while Jerry Falwell welcomed all comers to his non-sectarian Moral Majority, he rejected the fellowship of other Christians who did not adhere to his fundamentalist doctrine. Living with his own contradiction, Falwell would even deny his pulpit to Billy Graham because the evangelist consorted with Christians who did not qualify as fundamentalists. At the same time, he would not reject atheists who wanted to join the Moral Majority.

Theological contradictions aside, Jerry Falwell put social morality

back on the evangelical agenda for the 1980s. His public pronouncements made headline news in the late 1970s and early 1980s. Ronald
Reagan then milked the support of this grassroots network through
his platform espousing "traditional values." This extended the agenda of the Moral Majority to include other conservative, right-wing
issues, such as prayer in the public schools, supply-side economics
and a constitutional amendment prohibiting abortion. The irony
compounded. Jimmy Carter, the born-again Christian who came into
office on the evangelical vote, lost that same constituency at the polls
when public opinion swung radically to the right. This is not unusual.
Whenever a society is threatened by revolutionary change, particularly in the field of morals, the first reaction is to return to the ways that
worked in the past. Students of the Great Awakenings call this conservative swing a "nativist reaction." Not surprisingly, then, for the
next eight years of the Reagan presidency, other prophetic voices
were stilled and a Great Awakening seemed to be stalled by a nativist
return to traditional values.

The Nebulous Nineties: The Jury Is Still Out
*The critical test of a Great Awakening is whether or not it leads to
a new moral consensus, the necessary basis for social reform.* If this
test is applied to our society in the 1990s, a Great Awakening in the
twentieth century is either stalled, aborted or yet to come.

Back in 1976, when the born-again movement held center stage
in American life, church historian Martin Marty warned that it might
die like "bubble and fizz on the seashore." James Reston, a syndicated columnist, added his own concern when he asked the as-
sembled delegates at the 1980 Congress on the Laity if the born-again
movement would make a difference in the "moral pigsty" of American culture.

Has it happened? To date there is little evidence that the born-
again movement and the political action of evangelicals in the 1980s
have transformed our moral pigsty. Kenneth Kantzer, former editor
of *Christianity Today,* has written that moral corruption in the culture

actually increased in the 1980s.[9] Carl F. H. Henry adds his pessimism
in his book *Twilight of a Civilization: The Drift toward Neo-Paganism,*[10] and Charles Colson sounds his own dirge in the book
Against the Night: Living in the New Dark Ages.[11] At first glimpse, most ✳︎
of us would concur: greed dominates the marketplace; sex drives the
media; spills pollute the environment; racism is resurgent; economics divide the classes; drugs baffle our police; AIDS arouses our fears;
special-interest groups run our politics; and crime paralyzes our cities. Perhaps Colson is right when he says in his speeches, "We are
worshiping at the shrine of our darkest passions."

Well-known social analysts may not agree with the corruption of
the moral pigsty, but they certainly imply that the "moral throne is
empty."[12] Robert Bellah believes that Americans' *Habits of the Heart*
are shaped by radical self-interest rather than the common good.[13]
Studs Terkel sees the American landscape fractured by *The Great
Divide* between liberal and conservative factions with a spiritual void
in between.[14] Richard Neuhaus argues, in *The Naked Public Square,*[15]
that secular and religious forces are locked in mortal combat for
position. Robert Wuthnow believes that *The Struggle for America's
Soul* will be settled by a paradigm shift either to the left or the right.[16]

Thus I conclude, *if American history is written by great spiritual
awakenings, the twentieth century is still a shadowy blur.*

But let's not be too impatient with the present. We need to look
at past awakenings in more depth. In the next few chapters we will
see that one of the most important things to be learned from previous
Great Awakenings is that *it takes at least one generation or more for
the cycle of the Spirit to make a full revolution.* This means that the
1990s, not unlike the 1790s and the 1890s, may well be the decade
of destiny for our century. Again, if the pattern of history holds, a
Great Awakening in the twentieth century would be confirmed by an
outpouring of God's Spirit on Christian students on the college campus who see a redemptive vision for our moral pigsty.

2 | Heirs of a Haystack

*T*hey huddled under a haystack. Ordinarily the five college students met under the protective branches of a large maple tree and under the cover of night to read the Word of God, confess their sins, sing a song of forgiveness and pray for revival on their campus. Even the minutes of their meetings were kept in secret.

Tonight was different. The small, beleaguered company had been driven from their secret sanctuary by thunder that drowned out their prayers, lightning that crackled around them and rain that drenched them to the skin. An old barn with the comfort of a haystack became their refuge. There, with the storm symbolizing the hostility of their campus against them and their faith, they intuitively knew that their moment had come. God would answer their prayers. With the mysterious wind of his Holy Spirit, he would bring convicting and cleansing power to Williams College, a school founded through spiritual revival but now a seedbed for sin and skepticism. *A Great Awakening was on the way!*

The *time* was 1806, when our American ancestors struggled to establish the democracy that had been won in the War of Independence. The *place* was Williams College in Massachusetts, where Christian students had to meet in secret in order to avoid public ridicule. The *people* were a nondescript band of five students, who seemed to be too serious for their own good. As unlikely as the time, place and people may seem, one of the Great Awakenings in American history can be traced back to 1806 at Williams College when a thunderstorm drove five students to prayer while huddled under a haystack.[1] In fact: *American history can be written through its Great Awakenings.*

The First Great Awakening: Fueling Our Freedom

Whether they knew it or not, the students under the haystack were the heirs of an earlier awakening in our history before independence from England. Although the colonies of New England had been founded by Puritans, who led a disciplined life and shared a biblical vision for their new homeland, the natural erosion of sin and self-interest took its toll. Spiritually, the oncoming generation assumed that their salvation was secure no matter how they lived. Socially, a combination of political oppression, personal degradation and philosophical skepticism led the nation into a wilderness of despair. Notes of hope had a hollow ring, and the future boded worse than the tortured past.

Out of that wilderness came a prophetic voice. The Rev. Jonathan Edwards, a Puritan preacher in the tradition of John the Baptist, put out a call to personal repentance which eventually cost him his pulpit. Edwards's sermon "Sinners in the Hands of an Angry God," preached at Enfield, Connecticut, in 1741, still serves not only as a model of empowered preaching but also as a turning point in the history of Great Awakenings. With an eloquence honed by the Holy Spirit, Edwards depicted hell so vividly for his hearers that sinners, by eyewitness report, hung onto the pews with whitened knuckles for fear of sliding into the flames of hell that very moment! Revival followed, not just on the confession of sin, but on the promise of joy that Edwards also preached. He reported hundreds of conversions sealed by public confession among the churches of New England.

Awakening spread, however, under the impetus of a twenty-three-year-old itinerant preacher from England named George Whitefield. Fresh from the experience of the Evangelical Awakening in England where he had convinced John Wesley to take to the open fields for his preaching, Whitefield traversed the colonies—against the opposition of the Anglican clergy—to take the gospel to unchurched people. Benjamin Franklin, though an avowed deist, became a fast friend of Whitefield. Almost in awe, Franklin estimated that Whitefield's voice had the volume and the resonance to reach 30,000 people in the open fields. More amazingly, Benjamin Franklin built Whitefield a "preaching house" in Philadelphia, which gave him a pulpit for evangelism outside the Anglican Church. The "preaching house" later became the first building for the University of Pennsylvania. For us, however, it is even more notable that Whitefield had been a member, with John and Charles Wesley, of the Holy Club at Oxford University in the early 1730s. And although the Holy Club never left England, it is fair to say that this small group of Christian students had a share in the beginnings of the First Great Awakening in American history through the agency of its alumnus George Whitefield. Thousands were converted under his preaching. He became identified with Jonathan Edwards as one of the New Lights, who spoke prophetically of political freedom from the oppression of England as well as the spiritual freedom from the slavery of sin. The First Great Awakening came to its culmination when religion served as the vehicle for a moral consensus which could not tolerate the heavy hand of George II, king of England. *A Great Awakening fueled our freedom,* and the revolution that followed forever changed the course of our history.

 The Second Great Awakening: Ensuring Our Democracy
Spiritual awakenings usually take a full generation to work them-

selves through to a new moral consensus out of which social transformation is born. Likewise, the turn of just one generation under the catalyst of speeding social change can undo the moral consensus and kill the vitality created by a spiritual awakening.

The worst happened after we won our independence in 1776 and wrote our Constitution in 1789. In the aftermath of revolution, our forefathers forgot the spiritual roots from which their freedom sprang. Instead of returning to the biblical vision of the moral community which Governor Winthrop proclaimed to the Pilgrim band in a sermon just before they left the *Mayflower*,[2] the new generation of Americans identified with the seething caldron of infidelity and deism in prerevolutionary France. To say the least, the future of American democracy teetered in the balance, with the scales tipped toward anarchy.

Colonial colleges, in particular, took the brunt of moral corruption and philosophical despair. Harvard, Princeton and Yale, schools which were founded to prepare Christian leaders in religion, government and medicine, became seedbeds of atheism and anarchy. One historian of American higher education likened the climate of the college dormitories to "secret nurseries of every vice and the cages of unclean birds."[3]

Blasphemy followed heresy. In one college, students performed a mock communion with a parody of the sacred ritual at the chapel altar. In another, a deck of playing cards fell out of a hole cut in the pages of the president's Bible as he stood to address the students. In still another college, the students organized a drinking society with the name H.E.O.T.T. in parody of Isaiah's promise, "Ho, everyone that thirsteth." No wonder that any student who professed to be a Christian became the target for open ridicule and subtle discrimination. Quite in contrast with the evangelistic beginnings of the colleges, small bands of Christians now met in secret to pray.

Into this climate of corruption God called Timothy Dwight, grandson of Jonathan Edwards, to be the president of Yale in 1795. Fearlessly, Dwight chose his first baccalaureate sermon to invite all students to an open forum on the Christian faith. After hearing their attacks, he followed with a chapel series in which he spoke the "truth with love"—so much so that one-half of the Yale student body professed Christ before the year was out. One by one, spontaneous stirrings of the Spirit took place on college campuses.

Williams College, however, remained a hard-core center for heresy, blasphemy and ridicule—until the five students prayed under a haystack in 1806. With the mystery of the wind, the Spirit of God swept over the campus bringing repentance and redemption to scores of students who, in turn, took the witness of revival from campus to campus, church to church and city to city until "Awakening" became the watchword for the struggling nation. No one contests the genuine nature of that movement as infidelity gave way to vigorous faith and deism went bankrupt against the revelation of a personal God who loves and redeems all humankind.

Francis Asbury stands in rugged contrast to the image of the scholarly president of Yale or one of the cultured priests of the Anglican Church. Sent to America by John Wesley with the mandate "Offer them Christ," Asbury took his charge seriously by becoming a traveling Methodist preacher on the fast and ever-moving Western frontier. Enlisting impassioned and usually unlearned men, he created a mobile system of circuit-riders. Pastors on horseback, these men made the frontier their parish, establishing evangelistic outposts with camp meetings that reached thousands of people at a time.

Although Francis Asbury died in 1816, the momentum of his ministry was carried on by such a rough-and-tumble circuit rider as Peter Cartwright. In the book *The Democratization of American Christianity*, Nathan Hatch describes the genius of Asbury on the frontier as leading a "military mission of short-term agents"[4]—itinerant preachers armed with the gospel. Critics of Asbury scoffed when he built a church for Methodists, saying that the movement could be "contained in a corncrib." Later they had to eat their words. Between 1820 and 1830 alone, Methodism doubled in size to become one of the most formidable forces for spiritual regeneration and social reform on the American frontier.

Once again, the ideals and morals of the American people were turned upside-down. Alexis de Tocqueville, the French historian who chronicled our history in his classical work *Democracy in America,* expressed serious doubts that democracy could survive in the American experiment because freedom requires a moral base. He observed what we must not forget: *Democracy depends on a moral foundation of revealed truth mediated through religious institutions.*

In 1831 de Tocqueville visited the United States to observe first-hand our experiment in democracy. He found a transformed nation. The moral foundations of revealed truth were strong and the religious institutions were vigorous—evidence of a Great Awakening. At a barn-raising in Pennsylvania de Tocqueville saw the symbol of transformation. Neighbors from far and near voluntarily came to help another neighbor build a barn in one day. In the evening, they celebrated their achievement with supper and song. To de Tocqueville, the event represented democracy at its best. He went home to write, "America is a nation with the soul of a church." What began on a college campus became the energizing force that transformed a nation. *It took a Great Awakening to ensure our democracy.*

The Third Great Awakening: Building a Benevolent Empire

After the Great Awakening at the turn of the nineteenth century, another generation passed and America was in trouble again. As the new nation grew by spreading south and west, the unity of the 1820s was torn apart by the deepening hostility between the industrial North and the agricultural South. Slavery became the issue of freedom on which our democracy would again rise or fall. Not since the tumultuous days preceding the Great Awakening of the 1740s had the division been deeper and the conflict more volatile. The threat of secession by the southern states in the nineteenth century more than matched the threat of those who sided with the English king in the eighteenth century.

Although some historians are reluctant to identify the revival of the

1850s as a genuine Great Awakening, the long-term social and moral impact on the nation cannot be denied. An expanding network of intercessory prayer among businessmen, particularly in cities such as Philadelphia and New York, is usually cited as the source of the 1858 revival.[5] Skeptics, of course, suggest that the fervency of the prayers equaled the panic over a crumbling economy which threatened to bankrupt their businesses and lower their quality of life. Such skeptics fail to recognize the extension of those prayers beyond individual self-interest. Out of those prayer groups came the Young Men's Christian Association (YMCA), an organization founded to take the gospel to the campuses of the developing system of state universities and to serve the social, educational and spiritual needs of young men in the burgeoning cities of the nation.[6]

From that same extended motive came the full range of human-service agencies staffed by community volunteers, such as the United Way, the American Red Cross and the Young Women's Christian Association. These human-service agencies were complemented by political action that brought about enlightened changes in prison reform, child labor laws and women's rights. No wonder that America in the nineteenth century became known as "The Benevolent Empire"—another way of expressing de Tocqueville's observation that "America is a nation with the soul of a church." Although the spiritual roots of these voluntary agencies and policies of social reform may have been cut by future generations, their humanitarian motive had its origin in Christian compassion. Not by coincidence, community agencies serving human needs and staffed by volunteers are a phenomenon unique to American culture because they were born out of revival.

Again, the stir of awakening on college campuses preceded the revival of 1858. In the 1840s Charles Finney, an educator-evangelist, spoke as the president of Oberlin College, where students were in the midst of a campus revival. President Finney, not unlike Timothy Dwight of Yale, used the chapel platform to condemn the institution of slavery as antithetical to the spiritual freedom that the students found in Christ. The message and the spirit of revival sped from campus to campus and fueled the abolition movement with biblical meaning and evangelistic fervor. If a revival requires social reform to qualify as an Awakening, the Emancipation Proclamation leaves no doubt about the lasting impact of the Great Awakening that began on a college campus in the midst of revival. Gilbert Barnes, an historian of the anti-slavery movement, concludes: "In leadership, in method and in objective, the Great Revival and the American Anti-slavery Society now were one."[7]

Dwight L. Moody might well be called the Francis Asbury of the Third Great Awakening. Neither of them was schooled or sophisticated. Yet, under the impulse of the Spirit of God, they refused to recognize their limitations. As Asbury took the simple gospel to the Western frontier, Moody took the message of hope to the working people of the burgeoning industrial cities of the nation. As a role player in the Great Awakening, Moody did not preach social reform but rather said, "I look on this world as a wrecked vessel. God has given me a lifeboat and said to me, 'Moody, save all you can.' " Those who criticize his lack of substance or his flamboyant style forget the role he played as a voice in the "wilderness" of the urban frontier crying, "Repent."

Reconstruction following the Civil War not only involved the healing of the nation's wounds and the rise of industrial cities, but also the founding of hundreds of colleges identified with the evangelical sector of American Christianity. Admittedly, many were founded to protect denominational youth from the concocted demons of "atheism, infidelity, the slaveholder, and the Pope."[8] Still, these colleges kept alive the spirit of revival in the church and the promise of reform in the nation. Asbury College, for example, was founded in 1890 under the mandate for original Methodism in America, "To spread Scriptural holiness across the land and reform the nation." The integrity of this spiritual and social purpose still defines the mission of the evangelical Christian college as an agent of revival in the church and awakenings in the nation.

④ The Fourth Great Awakening: Embracing the World

In the 1890s another turn of the generations brought with it another time of decline and conflict in American culture. While we euphemistically remember the Gay Nineties as a decade of hedonistic happiness, the truth is that we were a troubled people. The Industrial Revolution had introduced a new materialism into the culture, which contradicted the self-giving attitude of volunteerism. "Robber barons" were accumulating massive fortunes, which accentuated the plight of the poor. Under the perceived threat of impoverished immigrants from Europe who flooded our shores, protective isolationism from world affairs became the policy of the day. Deep divisions developed among our people with the influx of scientific materialism and rationalism from the German universities, which directly challenged the validity of divine revelation, the doctrine of creation and the reality of Christian faith. Ethical and ideological differences again split the nation. Two divergent lines of spiritual movement can be drawn from the 1890s into the early years of the twentieth century. One line is more divisive than unifying. American theology got caught up in the rapture of German scholarship and its penchant for the science of higher criticism as applied to the Bible. Of course, when reason reigns supreme, revelation cannot stand. Operating on this assumption, higher criticism took up the search for the historical Jesus, demythologized the Gospels, and denied the nature of sin or the need for personal redemption.

Under such influence, a companion movement developed with a post-millennial vision of bringing the kingdom of God on earth through the redemptive influence of the Social Gospel. Walter Rauschenbusch, Harry Emerson Fosdick and Washington Gladden took the lead as the prophetic voices and eloquent advocates of the new Social Gospel from their national pulpits. Gladden, from his Congregational pulpit in Columbus, Ohio, preached, "If we want the nations of the earth to understand Christianity, we have got to have a Christianized nation to show them."[9] Not without significance, then, the symbol for their spiritual utopia as America entered the twentieth century was a new periodical named *The Christian Century.*

A second line of spiritual movement can be drawn from campuses in England to America in the 1890s and on into the twentieth century. In 1882 D. L. Moody spoke at Cambridge University in England. The evangelist might have been disheartened by the ridicule he received from the student body, but out of that meeting seven students responded to the call to give themselves wholly to the will of God. Gathering together, they called themselves the Cambridge Seven and can rightfully be linked with the Holy Club, the Haystack Prayer Meeting and the YMCA of earlier years. God answered their prayers by a visit of his Spirit, who gave them a vision of the unevangelized world and its multiplied millions. Providentially their vision connected with students at twenty state university campuses in the United States who had also banded together in prayerful submission to the Holy Spirit.

As their forces converged and connected with students on other campuses, the Student Volunteer Movement came into being as the forerunner for such groups as InterVarsity Christian Fellowship and the Student Mission Association. The list of student leaders who came out of a revival spirit on those campuses reads like a *Who's Who* of world missions: John R. Mott, E. Stanley Jones, Robert Wilder, Samuel Zwemer and Robert Speer. No one laughed when they spoke their watchword, "The evangelization of the world in this generation." Mott himself wrote, "Next to the decision to take Christ as the Leader and Lord of my life, the watchword has had more influence than all other ideals and objectives combined to widen my horizon and enlarge my conception of the kingdom of God."[10] His words were backed by the evidence that the watchword served as a motivating and mobilizing vision. To him and his college friends goes the credit not only for offering Christ to millions of people overseas but also for breaking the protective isolationism of America in the 1890s by making the connections with spiritual awakening around the world.

The Welsh revival in 1904 is the best example. When the Spirit of God moved through the masses of that nation of poor and illiterate miners, the conversions were so complete that the pit-ponies in the mines did not respond when given orders without the profanity of their masters. Even more notable, the Welsh revival illustrates the fact that whenever there is a true spiritual awakening, the leaders and the people become advocates for the poor by founding institutions to serve them and initiating legislation to protect them.

A sad note spoils the Fourth Great Awakening of the 1890s for evangelical Christians. Timothy Smith, a historian from Johns Hopkins University who wrote *Revivalism and Social Reform,* contends that evangelical Christians exemplified the unity of personal holiness and social holiness in the last half of the nineteenth century.[11] But if historians of the early twentieth century are right, evangelicals abandoned the field of social reform in order to avoid being identified with liberals who had, in turn, abandoned personal evangelism.[12]

Perhaps this is the reason why other historians deny the designation of "Awakening" to the period 1890-1920. Awakenings bring together people of common faith who reach out to embrace outsiders. The split between personal redemption and the Social Gospel as well as the separation between national and international evangelism created a chasm that has never been breached in the twentieth century. Still, if one must choose, there is more evidence of a Great Awakening among the students who believed that they could evangelize the world in their generation than for the scholars who promised to bring the kingdom of God to earth in twentieth-century America. While neither side accomplished their task, the Social Gospel is bankrupt while evangelizing the world is more realistic than ever before.

What conclusion can we draw from this hasty journey through two centuries of awakenings in American history? In the beginning we learned that the history of America can be written through the turning points of spiritual awakenings. Now we know that those awakenings often began and came full cycle among Christian students on college campuses. Especially in the Great Awakenings in the closing decade of each century, college students led the way in moral reform and world evangelism. Is it too much to expect that God will pour out his Spirit on all flesh in the 1990s? Will he begin with Christian students on the college campus? Will he bring the stirrings of the Spirit which we have seen in the last half of the twentieth century into the full cycle of a Great Awakening?

3 | *The Cycle of the Spirit*

*T*he Great Awakenings in American history are a favorite subject of historians, theologians and sociologists. Like the blind men describing an elephant by touch, awakenings are differently defined by the scholars' place of touch and point of view. Historians tend to read awakenings as renewal movements within the church and the culture. Not unlike Spengler's thesis that civilizations go through periods of rise and decline, they see the church as a social institution that pulsates between periods of exhaustion and renewal. Such a theory ties awakenings closely with the cyclical history of the culture and tends to deny or ignore any supernatural intervention.

Theologians who study awakenings in American history tend to touch the movements at the point of revival. J. Edwin Orr, an astute student of evangelical awakenings, makes no distinction between a revival and an awakening. Both are the result of "a movement of the Holy Spirit bringing about a revival of New Testament Christianity into the church of Christ and its related community."[1] While Orr neither ignores nor rejects the rising and falling pulse of the history, he locates the source of awakenings in the New Testament model of intercessory prayer, prophetic preaching and evangelistic outreach. Without doubt, Orr sees the supernatural visitation of the Holy Spirit as the reason and the hope for the awakenings of American history. Another observer adds: "Theologically considered, evangelical awakenings are possible while three facts remain in operation: the Word of God, . . . the Church of God, . . . and the Spirit of God."[2]

Sociologists touch the phenomena of awakenings at still another point. Neither the natural pulse-beat of history nor the supernatural visitation of the Holy Spirit guides their thoughts. Rather they see the awakenings as revitalization movements which are the result of a "deliberate, organized, conscious effort by members of a society to construct a satisfying culture."[3] Sociologist Anthony Wallace, father of the revitalization theory, offers a cultural cycle of five stages: (1) steady state; (2) individual stress; (3) cultural distortion; (4) revitalization; and (5) a new steady state. (As noted earlier, *steady state* means a period in time in a society when the moral consensus is strong, the established institutions of the home, the church and the school are stable, and legitimate leaders are accepted with confidence.)

Spiritual awakenings, then, take place during the revitalization states when religious movements *reformulate* the moral mazeways by which people live, *communicate* the new vision through prophetic leaders, *organize* the prophetic leaders, disciples and followers into a working unit, *adapt* the vision to the context of the culture, *transform* the culture according to the new vision and *institutionalize* the movement in new forms of ministry.

Although Wallace's revitalization theory needs no supernatural intervention, Christian scholars and theologians have found it helpful as a framework within which the cycle of the culture and the Spirit of God can be seen working together. Richard Lovelace, for instance, brings what he calls a "unified field theory" to the study of revival, renewal and awakenings. By blending biblical theology with components of cultural anthropology, he provides an integrated framework for viewing spiritual renewal as continuous, cyclical and supernatural. "Spiritual renewal is produced by the presence and empowering of the Holy Spirit; not simply by the comprehension of doctrinal propositions or strategies of renewal."[4]

Throughout the history of awakenings, the balance between *supernatural intervention* and *human initiative* has been a point of contention. Puritan theology, of course, left no doubt about the sovereignty of God in choosing the time, place and people for spiritual awakening. Jonathan Edwards lost his pulpit by preaching the necessity of personal repentance and public confession even within the doctrine of predestination. Peter Cartwright, the Methodist circuit rider, put even greater emphasis on individual decisions at a camp-meeting altar, and Charles Finney tipped the scales heavily toward human initiative in planning and organizing for revival and awakening. We should not be surprised then when Walter Rauschenbusch and Harry Emerson Fosdick abandoned the call for personal redemption and preached the Social Gospel as the hope for humankind.

> The individualistic concept of personal salvation has pushed out of sight the collective idea of a Kingdom of God on earth, and Christian men . . . are comparatively indifferent to the spread of the Spirit of Christ in the political, industrial, social, scientific and artistic life of humanity.[5]

Despite the differences that divide those who study awakenings in American history, Howard Snyder, in *Signs of the Spirit*, notes the concurrence among scholars that the life of the church rises and falls in an oscillating but similar pattern and that church history must be seen, "not in static, linear terms, but as dynamic, living, and fluctuating."[6] With Snyder, I would add the distinction of the work of the Holy Spirit and the Word of God in the process of revival, renewal and awakening. Accordingly, we can relate Wallace's revitalization theory with the evidence of God's Spirit moving with history and intervening in history to bring about awakening according to the cycle of the Spirit.

Cultural Conflict: Phase 1

Awakenings invariably begin in a time of cultural conflict. The cause may be a natural period of exhaustion and decline in the culture. When speeding social change creates moral disjunctures in the culture and makes the traditional ways of coping with change obsolete, a society is in trouble. In either case, malaise sets in, along with self-doubt and despair. The symptoms of cultural conflict are threefold: (1) the existing moral consensus breaks down; (2) the traditional authority of established institutions, such as the home, church and school, is rejected; and (3) the credibility of legitimate leadership is questioned.

Each of the awakenings in American history began in a time of trouble caused by moral conflict. In the First Awakening the moral issue was political; in the Second Awakening it was philosophical; in the Third Awakening it was social; and in the Fourth Awakening the conflict was theological. Admittedly, such designations are oversimplified, but they illustrate the moral conflict that caused disjuncture throughout the whole nation, from national leadership to grassroots. Social change with its resultant tension is not enough to stimulate the process of spiritual awakening. *In a Great Awakening, the cultural conflict must be moral and the social tension must be disruptive.*

Personal Conviction: Phase 2

Moral conflicts in a culture are never impersonal. The conflict creates its greatest stress on individuals. Mild to moderate stress can be handled by the stress-reduction mechanisms that are a part of every culture. For us, those mechanisms range from protest marches to personal counseling. When those mechanisms fail and the problem is recognized as morally based, personal stress can lead to spiritual conviction, which is a prerequisite for repentance and redemption.

In the process of a great awakening, spiritual conviction is absolutely essential. Whether it is sinners in the hands of an angry God or slaves under the whip of a brutal master, until traditional stress-reduction mechanisms fail and people acknowledge that God alone is the answer, there is no awakening.

In a Great Awakening, a new awareness of the holy and pure character of the Lord is present. Young people, in particular, are most vulnerable to the personal stress that comes from moral conflict. Not only are they susceptible because they are young and idealistic, but they serve as scapegoats for the sins of society. Every culture that is in decline finds occasion to blame its sins on rebellious youth, especially when they are on college campuses. The Spirit of God, however, works differently. Through the sensitivity of the young, stress becomes conviction, conviction leads to conversion and conversion brings a redemptive view for the troubled culture. As we observed with the Haystack Prayer Meeting, the "bottom of the bird cage" on the college campus brought the nation to have the "soul of a church."

Mass Conversion: Phase 3
Great Awakenings are never local or elitist. If the movement of God remains local, it may qualify as a revival in the church but not as an awakening in the culture. If the movement is limited to a certain class of people or to one generation, it hardly qualifies as a revival, to say nothing about an awakening. Rather, an awakening is a repeat performance of Pentecost, which was a multi-cultural, multi-generational, multi-ethnic, and multi-class phenomenon. Great Awakenings in American history are also like that. Although they may have begun among a handful of students on a college campus, among the hearers of a sermon in a church or among a few laypeople at a noontime prayer meeting, awakenings never stay local or limited. Awakenings are always democratic!

In each Great Awakening, God raised up prophets who cried out in the wilderness beyond established institutions or stable settings— George Whitefield in the fields of New England, Francis Asbury on the frontiers of the South and the West, Charles Finney in the developing cities, and D. L. Moody among the unchurched and unreached. Only Whitefield with his Oxford degree qualified as a learned man. Asbury, Finney and Moody lacked a formal education; yet each of them recognized the value of sound learning as an accompaniment to vital piety. Finney became the president of Oberlin College; Asbury and Moody gave impetus to distinguished institutions of higher education that still bear their name. Their ability to cross the lines between the classes and the masses symbolizes the spirit of awakening at its best. As the apostle Paul saw no distinction between Jew and Greek, bond and free, male and female, a Great Awakening has no distinction of age, sex, race, class, creed or ethnic origin.

Biblical Consensus: Phase 4

Great Awakenings progress in the cycle of the Spirit with the sound of prophetic voices. In such cases prophecy is not just a foretelling of the future but a rediscovery of the gospel in terms that are particularly relevant to the needs of the people at that point in time.

In the First Great Awakening the prophetic voices were called New Lights, in obvious contrast to the Old Lights, who insisted on addressing new problems with old values or what is called a nativist reaction. Quite naturally, whenever we are threatened by social change, our first impulse is to return to the values that worked under past circumstances of change. This nativist response is good because awakenings are not revolutions in which the values of the past are completely denied. Rather awakenings become a test of truth for old and new values. Some survive and some do not. Throughout our history, then, New Lights have not been radicals or "rootless rebels." Rather, New Light leaders have taken us back to our biblical roots—the true meaning of *radical*—and rediscovered the meaning of eternal truth for changing times.

In the First and Third Great Awakenings of the mid-eighteenth and mid-nineteenth centuries, prophetic voices related the biblical meaning of freedom to political oppression and human slavery. In the Second and Fourth Great Awakenings at the close of those centuries, the biblical concept of evangelism was applied first to the Western frontier and a century later to the missionary movement around the globe.

Howard Snyder, in his book *Signs of the Spirit,* puts the rediscovery of the gospel first among the factors that lead to renewal in the church and awakenings in the culture. He states that the nature of this rediscovery of the gospel may be *personal* renewal of believers, *corporate* renewal of the body of Christ, *conceptual* renewal of the vision for the church, *structural* renewal of the form of the church, or *missiological* renewal for the calling of the church.[7] Although renewal of the church may begin any one of these five ways, Snyder notes that renewal must become personal and corporate to be *genuine,* conceptual and structural to be *long-lasting,* and missiological to be *biblically dynamic.*

John Wesley serves as an example. Personally, he rediscovered the gospel when his heart was "strangely warmed" at Aldersgate Street in 1738 after years of spiritual search through the conceptual, corporate, structural and missiological avenues of the established church. Conceptual renewal followed as he began to preach "free grace in all; free grace for all." Wesley's personal and conceptual rediscovery of the gospel then became the lodestar for renewing the corporate identity, the structural form and the missiological calling of the church.

A similar pattern of renewal can be traced in the Great Awakenings in America. Jonathan Edwards's rediscovery of the gospel, which required individual repentance and public confession of faith, rattled the cage of old-line Calvinism personally and conceptually. George Whitefield complemented Edwards's rediscovery with field preaching that equally shook the corporate, structural and missiological meaning of the established church. *Renewal of the church by the "rediscovery of the gospel" may be only a beginning for a Great Awakening, but there will be no awakening without it.*

More often than not, the "new lights" of Great Awakenings are young people who are open to what scholars call a "paradigm shift" in their thinking about the gospel personally, conceptually, corporately, structurally and missiologically. George Whitefield, the field preacher; Peter Cartwright, the circuit rider; D. L. Moody, the crusade evangelist; and John R. Mott, the missionary statesman, were all in their twenties when their prophetic voices began to be heard. Although their message matured with their age, they are remembered for the clarity and consistency of their rediscovered gospel for the renewal of the church. Yet until their message became the base for an ideological shift toward a new moral consensus in the nation, awakening did not occur. As with all prophets, the social impact of their message outlived them.

In each of the awakenings we have already noted that it takes a full generation for the rediscovery of the gospel to provide a new moral consensus. For this reason, the Great Awakenings are recognized in spans of thirty years or more: 1740-1776, 1790-1820, 1840-1870 and 1890-1920. So, as a guiding principle for understanding future as well as past awakenings: *Look for young, prophetic voices who communicate a rediscovery of the gospel that will not only renew the church but rebuild a moral consensus to reform the nation.*

Social Transformation: Phase 5

The cycle of the Spirit is not complete until the society is transformed. To stop short of social transformation is to abort a Great Awakening. Periodically there may be revivals in parts of the nation and renewals in parts of the church, but we are short-sighted to assume that these visitations of the Spirit, in themselves, will transform the society in which we live. Most of our visions for changing the world are limited because we see the first three phases in the cycle of the Spirit—cultural conflict, individual stress and mass conversion—as complete in themselves. Our diagnosis of moral conflict in the culture is precise; our perception of individual stress as spiritual conviction is keen; and our prayers for the conversion of the masses are well placed. But then, we tend to lapse back into the nativist, or traditional, values. If prophetic voices arise with a rediscovery of the gospel that might lead to a new moral consensus, we close our eyes and stop our ears. If social reformation is proposed for existing institutions or infrastructures in terms of social justice rather than personal morality, we label the proposals as unbiblical or unpatriotic.

The results of Great Awakenings condemn such a short-sighted view of the work of God's Spirit in human history. Let Dennis Kinlaw, president of Asbury College, give us a Spirit-guided overview of the Great Awakenings in American history:

> The most beneficent influences in our society have found their inception in a moment when God acts. To a revived heart, truth becomes more than an idea. That is why the moral earnestness of revival converts had much to do with the abolition of slavery, the temperance movement, a growing concern for child welfare, medical aid for the sick, education for all, women's suffrage, the reclamation of the socially lost such as the prostitute and the criminal, and the giving of the gospel to those where its truth had never gone.[8]

Our day is no different. The *cultural conflict* over the issues of freedom and justice is just as intense as it was in the eighteenth and nineteenth centuries. The *individual stress* is more debilitating than ever. The need for *mass conversion* goes unanswered. The *moral consensus* is all but shattered, and the *social transformation* of our homes, churches, schools, government, business and media awaits a spiritual awakening.

The promise of Joel 2:28-32 is still ours. It has never been canceled. When God pours out his Spirit on all people, our sons and daughters will still prophesy, our young men and women will still see visions, and our old men and women will still dream dreams. Let Dr. Kinlaw remind us once again, "When God comes in a moment of quickening illumination, the results are large and the shadow long."[9] Dare we see such a moment and such results in the cycle of the Spirit for our generation? Perhaps the long shadow is already being cast.

4 | *The Campus: Center of Stress*

*C*ollege campuses are microcosms of our culture. At first thought, we might breathe a sigh of relief because American colleges and universities seem quiet compared to the 1960s; students are going about the serious business of getting an education. What appears on the surface, however, may not be as innocent as it seems, and what is rumbling just beneath the surface may be the prelude to eruption. In the 1990s our campuses will reveal a culture in conflict.

The Stress of Self-interest
If there is a prevailing moral consensus on the college campus today, it appears to be a commitment to self-interest. Students alone are not to be blamed. They are the heirs of a "Me generation" that began almost two decades ago. After the turbulent years of campus violence had exhausted themselves in the mid-1970s, college students turned inwardly toward one of two responses. They either became part of the born-again movement, which offered a spiritual solution for their

disillusionment, or they retreated into a protective shell of radical self-interest. Christopher Lasch, an intellectual historian, perceived the latter trend in 1978 when he wrote *The Culture of Narcissism.* Lasch accurately portrayed radical self-interest as a person's preoccupation with the "Radical Now" in time, the "Radical Self" in motivation and "Radical Happiness" in achievement.[1]

While a limited number of people read Lasch's more scholarly analysis of the trend, Robert Ringer's popular *Looking Out for Number One* set a record for longevity on the *New York Times* bestsellers index.[2] Ringer did not disguise his credo for self-interest: Negotiate all relationships on a scale that tips to your own self-interest. Psychologists dignified the blatant self-interest of Ringer by developing equity theory, which also assumes that all human transactions are negotiated on the balance of self-interest. Pressed to its logical conclusion, equity theory leaves no room for genuine altruism. In every case there is a trade-off of values so that even a martyr will not die unless some equitable self-interest is served.

Such radical self-interest proved to be a short, dead-end street. By the 1980s the end was in view. Daniel Yankelovich, in his book *New Rules: Living in a World Turned Upside Down,* interpreted the results of his research survey to mean a shift toward an "ethic of commitment" by the members of the Me generation.[3] According to Yankelovich, as the Me generation aged into their thirties, they wanted to retain their self-interest and gain the values of warm, human relationships.

With just a slight shift toward an interest in others, human transactions in marriage or career took on the character of a "giving/getting contract."[4] Whether a pre-nuptial agreement, an employment contract or a community commitment, all relationships were negotiated on adversarial and legalistic terms to assure that *neither party gives more than one gets.* In the early 1980s Yankelovich saw revisions being made in the giving/getting contract as people also tried to incorporate their yearnings for human commitment into their experiment in self-fulfillment.[5] In other words, the Me generation wanted to be the We generation without giving up too much self-interest.

Robert Bellah does not buy into the alleged transition from the "Me" to the "We" generation. *Habits of the Heart*, written in 1985, may well be the most significant book of the decade. Based on interviews of young adults across the nation, Bellah concludes that our American character is being shaped by radical individualism at the expense of the "moral community" or the "common good." Two kinds of self-interest are identified: utilitarian individualism and expressive individualism.[6] In essence, utilitarian individualism means *doing what we want to do for our own profit,* and expressive individualism means *being what we want to be for our own pleasure.*[7]

Bellah sees these forces personified in three professional roles that we now extol as models for our culture and especially our students: the *entrepreneur,* who exploits resources in ventures of self-interest; the *manager,* who manipulates resources to serve the system at the expense of people; and the *therapist,* who makes us feel good about doing what we want to do for our own profit and being what we want to be for our own pleasure.

These models are not limited to secular leaders. Not long ago I received a brochure for recruiting a new president for a prominent Christian organization. Under the qualifications for the position, priority was given to a person who could inspire others with a creative vision, make tough decisions on programs and people to reduce a deficit, and raise morale with warm, participatory leadership. As I read the brochure I exclaimed, "There it is! Even in a Christian organization we want an entrepreneur, a manager and a therapist all rolled into one."

If religious prophets had said what Robert Bellah has written, they would have been ignored or crucified. Bellah's credibility as a leading scholar puts the ring of authority in his book, especially among professors and students on the college campus. The question is whether or not anyone has heeded his prophetic warning.

By the time we entered the 1990s, every major institution reeled under the impact of self-interest. In the *home,* the traditional nuclear family of two parents and children represented only 11 per cent of the households in the nation. In *business,* the greed of junk bonds, program trading, unfriendly take-overs and the savings and loan fiasco became a national disgrace. In *government,* ethics committees worked long and hard on multiple cases without either bark or bite; and in the *church,* a succession of infightings and sex scandals shook public confidence.

Radical self-interest also contaminated the college campuses, but in a less dramatic fashion. Perhaps the most alarming signal came from the American Council of Education (ACE) surveys of the college aspirations of incoming freshmen. In 1968, when the ACE surveys began, 70 per cent of the entering freshmen aspired to the goal of developing a philosophy of life as the outcome of their college career. Less than 40 per cent envisioned college as an opportunity to become well-off financially. Twenty-two years later the statistics were reversed for the entering class of 1990. Seventy per cent aspired to become well-off financially and less than 40 per cent were primarily interested in developing a philosophy of life.[8]

Careerism, another indicator of the aspiration to become well-off financially, leads students in their choices of fields of study in the 1990s. Ever since the mid-1970s students have traded majors in liberal arts for professional degrees in fields such as business, computer science and communications. The trend still holds in the 1990s, although there is some evidence of a small renaissance in some fields of liberal arts. By and large students still opt for "cash cows" in their college careers.

Of course, the trend away from the liberal arts and toward professional studies is not new. More disturbing is the underlying attitude of students. Frank Newman conducted the study *Higher Education and American Resurgence* for the Carnegie Foundation for the Advancement of Teaching in 1985. His findings indicted both our colleges and our culture. In his summary Newman noted that students were:

☐ choosing narrow, technical fields rather than the liberal arts;

☐ thinking in narrow, technical terms rather than asking philosophical questions;

☐ electing safe courses at a time when we needed leaders who were willing to take a risk; and

☐ becoming more parochial just when the position of the United States hung in the balance.

How does Newman account for his findings? He states: "By every measure that we have been able to find, today's graduates are less interested in and less prepared to exercise their civic responsibilities."[9]

Not just world affairs, but community affairs suffered from self-interest. Newman found that students were no more ready to assume leadership in the local community than they were on the world scene.

The most scathing indictment of the intellectual, cultural and moral climate of the campus, however, came from the philosopher Alan Bloom in his widely read volume *The Closing of the American Mind.* Although he is an agnostic Jew and avowed humanist, Bloom identifies the problem on campus as the loss of absolute truth as the ground for intellectual inquiry, moral integrity and cultural vitality. His opening sentence reveals the rationale for his book: "There is one thing a professor can be absolutely certain of; almost every student entering the university believes, or says he believes, that truth is relative."[10]

Once it is accepted that truth is relative, Bloom says, anything goes on the campus. Quite in contrast with the fear that their minds will be closed to truth, he characterizes the contemporary college student as a person who is "open to indifference"—accepting anything and indifferent to everything. In the absence of absolute truth, he argues, there are no standards for scholarly pursuit, cultural excellence, community values or personal integrity. Regrettably, Bloom's diagnosis is better than his prescription. Finding truth in the absolutes of Platonic idealism, he calls for a renaissance of community on campus in pursuit of those ideals.

College campuses are also the moral testing grounds for the larger culture. While frequently accused of being morally lax, the college campus actually reflects, often in advance, the changing morals of the society. At the opening of the 1990s, for example, colleges were debating condom dispensers, drug testing and date rape. At the same time students reversed earlier trends toward free sex, pot parties and alcohol bashes. Moral trends on campus are always unpredictable. The moral temperature of the campus climate cannot be easily forecasted. A recent resurgence of racism is another example. Except for the suspicion that racial prejudice continues as an undertow in the larger culture, we would not expect it to break out first on the campus. Despite its unpredictable nature, we cannot call the college campus of the 1990s the "bottom of a bird cage" or a "moral pigsty." More appropriately, *the college campus in the 1990s is a simmering stew of self-interest.*

Evangelical Christian students are not exempt from the subtle influence of self-interest. James Davison Hunter, in his book *Evangelicalism: The Coming Generation,* reports on the attitudes and values of students on Christian college and seminary campuses. The results may be gratifying or disturbing, depending on your priorities. Evangelical Christian students, for example, are distinctly different from their counterparts in public universities in matters of morals, such as premarital sex, homosexuality and cheating on income taxes, but merge with the general population of students in work values and goals of self-realization. Similar shifts in attitudes toward family, politics and world affairs lead Hunter to conclude:

> The caricature of evangelicalism as the last bastion of the traditional values of discipline and hard work for their own sake, self-sacrifice and moral asceticism, are largely inaccurate. Far from being untouched by the cultural trends of the post-World War II decades, the coming generation of evangelicals, in their own distinct ways, have come to participate in them.[11]

Past and present generations of evangelical Christians show another contrast. In matters of theology—such as biblical inerrancy, creationism and the particularity of salvation only in Jesus Christ—evangelical students are definitely more liberal than their parents and grandparents.

Although the value of Hunter's specific findings may be disputed by the questions he asked, his perception of the coming generation of evangelical Christians is well taken. Likening the young evangelical of today to Christian in Bunyan's *Pilgrim's Progress*, Hunter foresees this picture of the future:

> Though still headed toward the Celestial City, he (or she) is now travelling with less conviction, less confidence about his path, and is perhaps more vulnerable to the worldly attractions encountered by Bunyan's pilgrim.[12]

If so, evangelical Christian students on college campuses join with the culture in need of a Great Awakening. Hunter's call for a "new paradigm" for evangelical Christianity echoes the need for prophetic voices in the 1990s as the next phase of a Great Awakening. As a microcosm of a culture in which radical self-interest is shaping our character, hollowing our institutions, desacralizing our morals and twisting our values, *only a Great Awakening can reverse the trends*. It began on the campus in the 1790s and 1890s. Can it begin there again?

C. Robert Pace, professor of higher education at UCLA, believes it can. At the conclusion of his book *Education and Evangelism*, written for the Carnegie Commission on Higher Education, this social psychologist writes,

> Together with some awakening of spirit, and with a respect for experience and meaning that comes from both heaven and earth, our society may ensure the diversity of its education, the plurality of its culture and the Christian part of its heritage.[13]

A secular prophet has spoken. If he foresees our hope in "some awakening of spirit . . . that comes from both heaven and earth," why can't we?

5 | The Student: Candidate for Conversion

When God's Spirit is poured out on all people, it is no accident that the young see visions. Nor is it an accident when the stirring of the Spirit that leads to a Great Awakening begins on the college campus. Youth is a choice time of life when special gifts are in full bloom. Never again will a person be so *sensitive* to cultural conflict, so *optimistic* about the future, so *open* to the Spirit, so *energized* for action, and so *ready* to die for Christ. Perhaps the apostle Paul had these qualities in mind when he told Timothy, "Don't let anyone look down on you because you are young" (1 Tim 4:12) and "Stir up the gift of God which is in you" (2 Tim 1:6 NKJV). The two admonitions apply to Christian youth in every generation. College students, in particular, personify the gifts of youth. College students should never be despised, always stirred and, when visited by the Spirit and honored with God's vision for the future, they should be recognized as agents for a Great Awakening.

Sensitivity to Conflict

As cultural conflict comes to focus on the campus, college students become the subjects of that stress. Caught in the crossfire between the emotions of the teen-age years and the expectations of adulthood, a college student must respond to the bombardment from both sides. Yet college students neither have the excuse of adolescence nor the luxury of a mature, responsible adult who learns to handle conflict by separating the stress into physical, emotional and spiritual compartments. College students have a sensitivity to conflict resulting from stress that impacts their whole being, including their spiritual well-being.

Early in the 1980s I spoke in a college chapel on the subject "To Belong, To Be Loved, To Be Praised." My text was God's affirmation of his Son at Jesus' baptism, "You are my Son, whom I love; with you I am well pleased" (Mk 1:11). As I spoke about our loving God who adopted us as his sons and daughters, I revealed for the first time in public the trauma of my relationship with my father. Dad was my hero throughout my childhood and early teens, especially because of his example of faith in Jesus Christ. But the time came when communication between my parents swung from weeks of sullen silence to nights of angry screams. Finally the day came when my father told me that he was leaving my mother and added the barb that he had married my mother only to give me a name. Stunned, I could only blurt out the question, "But Dad, what about Christ?"

Dad answered, "I never knew him."

As I told my story, I wept and others wept with me. After the chapel I had an overwhelming response from students that I couldn't handle. In seeing me reveal my wounds, they began to see theirs as well. Student after student came to me with stories of marital conflict, broken homes, child abuse, parental estrangement and, in every case, a desperate need for reconciliation. Although I've avoided retelling the story for fear that it will become a tool for manipulation, whenever the Spirit has prompted me to tell it, the response is the same. *Both Christian and secular students are wounded people, sensitive victims of cultural conflict and domestic stress.*

The decade of the 1990s has not brought relief to students under stress. On the contrary, the emotional baggage that students bring to the campus has become so heavy that the premises underlying student development have had to be revised. In the past student development programs are designed to help a relatively healthy adolescent put all of the pieces of personal and interpersonal relationships together. Now a new prior assumption guides student services on the campus: The majority of incoming students come from dysfunctional families. Campus counselors spend the lion's share of time providing therapy for abuse and alcoholism, anorexia and AIDS, and sex and suicide. Remedial programs for emotional and relational deficiencies have become a major function for college, university and even seminary campuses. A culture in conflict has "bumped up" its stress to the college level. Although it's an unfair drain on academic resources, parents and students have made stress-reduction through counseling services a moral obligation of the campus in the 1990s.

The bad news has a good side. Because college students do not isolate their emotional stress from its spiritual implications, they are also sensitive to the prompting of God's Spirit in conviction for sin. But this will happen only if sin is identified as sin and not as "abuse," "addiction" or "codependency." John Guest, the evangelist and folk singer, parodies the psychology that blames our sin and sickness on our background in a ditty written by an unnamed psychiatrist:

I went to my psychiatrist to be psychoanalyzed,
To find out why I killed the cat and blacked my wife's eyes.
He laid me on a downy couch to see what he could find,
And this is what he dreg-ged up from my subconscious mind.

When I was one my mommy locked my dolly in the trunk,
And so it follows naturally that I am always drunk.
When I was two I saw my father kiss the maid one day.
That is why I suffer now from kleptomania.

When I was three I suffered from ambivalence toward my brothers.
That is just the reason why I poisoned all my lovers.
I'm so glad since I have learned that lesson that I've been taught,
That everything I do that's wrong is someone else's fault.

Hey, Libido,
Bats in the belfry,
Jolly ole Sigmund Freud.

It is particularly distressing to note that evangelical Christianity has
bowed at the shrine of counseling and psychotherapy. While best
sellers on psychospiritual self-help dominated the evangelical book
market in the 1970s and 1980s, it took two prominent psychiatrists
to remind us of our sinful nature. Karl Menninger wrote *Whatever
Happened to Sin?* [1] and Scott Peck followed with *People of the Lie:
The Hope for Healing Human Evil* [2] Not to be ignored is the fact that
Peck's most popular book, *The Road Less Traveled,* [3] which mingles
his psychoanalytical credentials with his religious faith, continues to
be among the most widely read books on the secular campus ten
years after its initial publication. *Sensitive students in spiritual search
are ready candidates for conviction and conversion.*

Optimistic about the Future
*Not even the heavy weight of personal stress discourages the gift of
idealism that God gives to the young.* Adults are not so optimistic.
After a period of time, our youthful visions are blunted by reality and
conditioned by compromise. The young, however, do not suffer such
handicaps. In the natural cycle of maturation, a college-age student
momentarily sees an "all-or-nothing" world of justice, love, freedom
and faith.

   During the protest days of 1970 Charles Reich wrote *The Greening
of America,* in which he likened idealistic youth to a flower that grows
up through a crack in the concrete and blossoms with glory against
its hardened and lifeless surroundings. [4] The concrete, of course, sym-

bolized the "system" and the flower represented students, who were the only hope in a dead society. Perhaps he drew the analogy from the flowers these "flower children" carried. But like a cut flower, they bloomed for only a short time because their romantic idealism lacked the roots of moral substance for sustaining its life.

Youthful idealism will invariably go the way of the "flower children" unless it is rooted in spiritual substance. As Howard Snyder has already informed us, a renewal movement must be both personal and conceptual if it is to be genuine. Otherwise, when the bubble-and-fizz of youthful passion disappears, nothing is left.

The stirrings of the Spirit in the vision of college-age Christians has had that rootedness. Compare the Cambridge Seven of the 1890s, who were the forerunners of a Great Awakening, with the Chicago Seven of the 1960s, who broke up the Democratic party's national convention. Every member of the Cambridge Seven followed his lofty vision of world evangelization to some mission outpost for a lifetime. When the Chicago Seven held its twentieth reunion in 1988, however, every member had either re-entered the system against which he rebelled or continued to wander as a "burnout" in the aftermath of revolution.

The idealism of the young is a gift of God that can be either infused with a substantive, long-term vision of the future or abused as a momentary, reactionary protest. A Great Awakening in the 1990s depends on the Truth of the ages being blended with the optimism of the young to give us the Spirit-filled vision of the future that commands our commitment. When the Cambridge Seven put their optimism into the watchword "The evangelization of the world in this generation," they gave us a vision that did not die.

Openness to the Spirit of God

College students have another advantage which is often lost with age. *They are open to the outpouring of the Spirit of God no matter what form it takes and through whatever avenues it flows.* For this reason, a revival among students on a college campus is often discounted as youthful enthusiasm. In the eighteenth century John Wesley and his friends at Oxford University had to live with the derisive label "Holy Club," even though they were chided as "Methodists" at the same time.

Adults are not so flexible. On a college campus recently a student leader responded enthusiastically to my lecture entitled "Welcome to the Awakening" by reporting how he had been baptized by the Holy Spirit, spoken in tongues and cast out demons. Reactive hairs on the back of my neck stood straight up. As an adult who had been reared in the Holiness tradition without tongues and as a psychologist who had defined demons in terms of psychosis, my first impulse was to reject the authenticity of his experience.

But then I choked on my own words. In the chapel address I had urged the students to be open to the stirrings of the Spirit, however they may come and wherever they may be. Who then was I to deny the unusual manifestation of the Spirit in this young man? So I shifted from negative body language to a positive reinforcement of his experience, though I urged him to undergird his leadership with serious study of the Word of God and the disciplines of his field of study.

Great Awakenings which have begun among college students have baffled observers who expected emotional excesses. Because young people are open to the Spirit, their revivals are never without enthusiasm. At the same time, nevertheless, their emotions surge within the channels of the Spirit so that even skeptics lose their case. As a reporter from the *Chicago Tribune* wrote on the front page of the Sunday paper after visiting Anderson College during its campus revival in 1970:

> The revival has made a splash that is sending ripples throughout the country. . . . Many people who came prepared to be skeptical at the emotional nature of the meetings have been impressed with the sincerity and the contagious atmosphere of the sessions. . . . In a day when many congregations are worried about losing their appeal to young people, Anderson's "Revival of Love"

seems to be saying something.[5]
There is nothing to fear from college students who are open to the Spirit because they are as open to his governance as they are to his fervor.

Energized for Action

Energy flows through open channels when God pours out his Spirit on the young. No one disputes the fact that college-age people are at the peak of their physical, sexual, intellectual and social energies. For these young adults, "Just Do It" is more than a clever advertising slogan. Time and time again we have heard young achievers, from Miss America to the Heisman Trophy winner, say, "You can do anything you want to do." They may not be right, but they have the energy to try.

Adults are just the opposite. We put most of our energy into hours of strategic planning, which carefully accounts for environmental threats and opportunities as well as institutional strengths and weaknesses in order to arrive at our priorities. When planning is translated into tactics we assess the available resources of people, money, time and space to reach our desired outcomes. Most often, however, strategic planning is an exercise in futility because the plans fill volumes while the results hardly cover a memo pad.

Young people put a premium on action, with a minimum of planning. This is both their strength and their weakness. The weakness is exposed when the action backfires; but the strength is revealed when they get the right things done. With only a vision of the Spirit to guide them, young leaders of the Great Awakenings have won freedom for our nation, ensured democracy in America, freed the slaves and set out to evangelize the globe. Their energized action reminds me of the college student who stepped off into a faith mission with nothing more than the promise "If God is in it, it will flow." No wonder that God honors the young with visions. They have the motivation and the energy to go with the flow and see those visions become reality.

Ready to Die

When our youngest son, Rob, criticized a church service we attended, he said, "Dad, the passion is missing." Youthful passion is far more than sexual energy. *When the passion of the young is set ablaze by the outpouring of the Spirit, they are ready for self-sacrifice, even ready to die for their faith.*

How do I know? Once, on another college campus, I took the risk of speaking to students on Paul's spiritual regimen, "I die daily" (1 Cor 15:31 KJV). I began by sharing the results of a survey on self-interest, which shows its dominance as a life motive today. I sensed that the students were right with me when I quoted the young swinger who summed up her self-seeking life the morning after as "dirty bed sheets and a mouthful of ashes." Turning then to the incarnational self-sacrifice of Jesus as described in the second chapter of Philippians, I called them to be of the "same mind" as Christ by daily dying to self. My examples came from Vernon Grounds's chapter on "Daily Self-Death" in *Radical Commitment*. Dr. Grounds noted that Mildred Cable, missionary to China; George Mueller, the man of prayer; and Frank Laubach, the missionary statesman, all arrived at the moment in their spiritual journey when they said, "That night I died." Once dead to self, however, God honored them with fruitful ministries that still serve as models for us today.[6]

After that chapel students lined up to ask me for the name of the book and its author so that they could read the chapter for themselves. Through the Spirit I had touched another chord that resonates among college students today. Unfortunately, we adults often project on them our drive to save ourselves and our desire for a comfortable life. The truth is that college students are witnesses to the dead-end of radical self-interest and are now ready to take seriously Jesus' hardest saying of all: "For whoever wants to save his life will lose it, but whoever loses his life for me will find it" (Mt 16:25).

No doubt remains why God gives visions to the young when he pours out his Spirit on all people. With the gift of youth comes sensitivity to conflict, optimism for the future, openness to the Spirit, energy for action and a readiness to die. Young people in the 1990s are no different. *We can rightfully expect a Great Awakening to begin on the college campus among Christian students.*

6 | *The Cell: School for Spirituality*

Great *Awakenings have small beginnings. In one way or another* the impetus for awakening comes from a handful of students bonded together in a small group and praying for revival. Mark Hopkins, missionary-educator who became president of Brown University, recognized the genius and power of such a group when he dedicated a plaque in 1867 at the site of the Haystack Prayer Meeting. He said, "For once in history a prayer meeting is commemorated by a monument."[1]

The Golden Link
Later, when the history of the YMCA was written, its author noted that the cell groups on college campuses formed a "golden link" stretching from the Haystack Prayer Meeting in 1806 to the student missions movement in the 1890s. These groups included the College Praying Society at Brown, the Harvard Saturday Evening Religious Club, the Yale Student Moral Society, the YMCA chapter on the University of

Michigan and the Princeton Foreign Mission Society.[2] According to C. Howard Hopkins this chain of groups led to the "greatest student uprising in all history"—referring to the student missions movement that began in the Great Awakening of the 1890s and spread throughout the world.[3] At the end of the twentieth century we can see that same golden link stretching back to the Holy Club at Oxford in the 1700s and forward to the prayer bands at Asbury in the 1970s. But is he right that the greatest student uprising is in the past? Or is it yet ahead? *The answer lies in the golden link of history that extends to cell groups on campus in the 1990s.*

Forging the Golden Link

Cell groups arise out of felt need. In the 1790s, when college campuses were becoming increasingly corrupt, and in the 1890s, when they were becoming increasingly secular, Christian students banded together in small groups as a beleaguered minority. Their numbers were so small that only a handful of students met in secret to give each other *personal support.*

I know a bit how they felt. The chaplain of a college that had been founded out of revival in the late 1800s begged me to give a lecture series on campus in support of his fledgling ministry. I went with low expectations, which fell further after I arrived. Three students met with the chaplain and me in the empty and rundown Center for Campus Ministry. As we reviewed the plans for the lecture that I would give the next day, the students apologetically informed me that they could count only 12 students out of an enrollment of 500 who professed to be Christians. "Don't expect more than that number at the lecture tomorrow," they advised. "Attendance is optional."

A class in oral communication, which came to criticize my lecture as a course requirement, saved the day. Twenty-five students made up my audience. That night the 5 of us prayed and attendance on the second day rose to 75. We prayed again and 125 students showed up for the concluding lecture. The president thanked me for coming with a backhanded compliment, "At this rate, if we could keep you speaking long enough, we might get the whole student body to attend." Although the results of that lecture series may have been minimal, I count my ministry of encouragement for that chaplain and Christian students among my most rewarding memories. I identified not only with the small cell that met each day to pray for revival on that campus but also with the student prayer cells throughout history that have been catalysts for spiritual awakenings under the most trying of circumstances.

One day while studying the Gospel of Mark, I realized that Jesus needed a cell group of twelve disciples for personal support. We remember that he called the Twelve and ordained them "that he might send them out to preach and to have authority to drive out demons" (Mk 3:14). But we miss the first and prior purpose of their calling: "that they might be with him." Jesus knew that he would need their support in times of triumph as well as in times of tension. His need for friends confirms how much more we need each other.

Complementing the need for personal support, student cell groups also met for the purpose of *spiritual discipline*. Members not only supported each other but pledged themselves to mutual accountability for spiritual growth. Regular, punctual and methodical meetings followed a pattern of penetrating questions on the spiritual state of the members, confession of sin, submission to the Word of God, intercessory prayer, fasting and songs of celebration. The Holy Club at Oxford in 1733-1734 serves as an example:

The members of the Club spent an hour, morning and evening, in private prayer. At nine, twelve and three o'clock they recited a collect, and at all times they examined themselves closely, watching for the signs of grace and trying to preserve a high degree of religious fervor. They made use of pious ejaculations, they frequently consulted their Bibles, and they noted, in diaries, all the particulars of their daily employment. One hour each day was set aside for meditation. . . . They fasted twice a week, observed all the feasts of the Church, and received the Sacraments every Sunday. Before going into company they prepared their conversation, so that the words might not be spoken without purpose. The Primitive Church, in so far as they had knowledge of it, was to be taken as their pattern.[4]

We react against this kind of regimentation for three reasons. First, we remember the futility with which a person such as John Wesley sought holiness through spiritual discipline and failed. Without the dynamic of a heartwarming experience of grace such as Wesley experienced at Aldersgate in 1738, no spiritual discipline can help us. Second, as members of a self-indulgent age, we feel that rigorous spiritual discipline is alien to our existence. Yet, deep down, we know that our flabby faith is symptomatic of our soft spiritual life. Third, in keeping with our secularized Western mind, we depend on Christian activism for the development of our spirituality. As Americans, we believe, "If anything can be done, it must be done."

Consequently, we are a generation of spiritual doers who do not have the time or patience to exercise the spiritual disciplines of "being." As an evangelical activist myself, I realize that our board meetings, strategy sessions and staff retreats minimize prayer and maximize planning. Evidently we assume that our spiritual "being" is a private matter while our spiritual "doing" is a corporate responsibility. Jesus' example of working with his disciples and Paul's emphasis on the body of Christ refute this notion. Our "being" and "doing" require mutual accountability in the Christian community as well as personal accountability to God.

To personal support and spiritual disciplines, the student cell groups added an emphasis on *social compassion*. Going back to the religious societies of the 1700s again, Snyder notes that their members "visited the poor at their houses and relieved them, fixed some in the way of trade, set prisoners at liberty, and furthered poor scholars at the University and established scores of charity schools for the poor."[5] Although the so-called Holy Club at Oxford varied from the religious aid societies in matters of personal piety, from its very beginning the members took it on themselves to visit the poor and prisoners. Later, when John Wesley organized "bands" and "societies" for the nurture of his converts, he set the requirement that each member give a penny to the poor each week, even if they were among the poor themselves.

College student cells throughout American history were begun for the purposes of personal support and spiritual discipline and invariably moved to some expression of social compassion. Samuel J. Mills, for example, whom we remember as the student leader of the Haystack Prayer Meeting, made no distinction between home and foreign missions or between evangelism and social service. In 1816, the same year that Mills participated in the founding of the American Bible Society, he worked for the summer in the ghettos of New York City among poverty-stricken people and at the docks with down-and-out sailors.

Naturally then, the spiritual motivation for cell groups progressed from *social compassion* to *world evangelism*. Here the history of the Great Awakening of the 1890s is written large. David Howard makes that history come alive in his book *Student Power in World Evangelism*. In grand succession, the Awakening produced the Student Volunteer Movement for Foreign Missions, the World Student Christian Federation, the Student Foreign Missions Fellowship, InterVarsity Christian Fellowship and the Urbana World Missions Conference. Although these organizations have risen, changed and sometimes declined with the pulse beat of the culture and the campus, their missiological motivation has continued for a full century as a testimonial to a Great Awakening.

Four sequential purposes, then, forge the link in the golden chain of student cell groups: *personal support* for new believers; *spiritual discipline* for maturing members; *social compassion* for the poor; and *world evangelism* for the unreached. Where does intercessory prayer for revival on the campus come in? Perhaps it is infused throughout each purpose as the members demonstrate the meaning of their faith. Or perhaps it is an essential part of spiritual discipline. In either case, we know from history that campus revival, church renewal and cultural reform—the evidence of a Great Awakening—do not happen by chance. Although God chooses the "fullness of time" when he pours out his Spirit, his time in history is always filled up with the prayers of his people.

Connecting the Golden Link

From the campus cells of the past we can learn some lessons for reviving those cells on the campus today.

1. *Keep each cell small.* It is amazing to learn how few members there were in the most effective cell groups in the history of Great Awakenings—four in the Holy Club and five in the Haystack Prayer Meeting. In each case the members were intensely motivated to fulfill the avowed purposes of the cell. Peter Drucker, the "father" of management consultation, says, "You can't motivate the masses." Although he is referring to large-scale organizations, the converse is also true, "The smaller the group, the greater the motivation."

2. *Keep the membership dynamic.* All groups have a natural tendency to become comfortable and cliquish. To avoid such in-grown stagnation, new believers should be brought into the group constantly, and new cells should be spun off when an agreed-on maximum is reached. Vitality in a cell group is assured by the introduction of new believers. Their questions are always pointed and their answers are always fresh. A new believer who had a Roman Catholic background accepted an invitation into my wife's prayer and Bible study group. Suddenly, my wife reported that they quit talking to each other in evangelical clichés because she kept asking, "What do you mean by that?" The women in the prayer cell ended up learning as much or more from her than they ever taught her.

3. *Establish a plan for mutual accountability.* Without a common commitment to mutual accountability, a cell group will become nothing more than a forum in which the members protect themselves by talking around the life-and-death issues of spirituality. Any campus cell group will be revolutionized by the kind of questions that the members of the Holy Club asked each other every week:

☐ Do you desire to flee the wrath to come?

☐ Do you have known sin in your life?

☐ Are you at peace with your brothers and sisters?

☐ Do you have the witness of the Spirit now that you are a child of God?

While the questions we ask may be phrased in more contemporary language, the content would be the same. As Henri Nouwen warns us, one of the temptations into which Christians so frequently fall is the temptation *to go solo.*[6] Most of the scandals of Christian leaders and the defections of Christian disciples are avoidable if only we had a system of face-to-face accountability in which all Christians participated.

4. *Rely on the authority of the Word of God as the checkpoint for the purposes of the cell.* Again, a natural tendency of a group is to overbalance the emphasis on one function of a cell: personal support, spiritual discipline, social compassion or world evangelism. The history of a group such as the YMCA serves as a warning that social compassion born out of revival can be diluted into humanitarian services unless the roots of the movement are constantly fed by revealed truth.

Or the opposite can happen. Evangelicals in the early 1900s forfeited the field of social compassion to liberals and retreated into a gospel of personal piety and world evangelism, sending scores of missionaries overseas. If the authority of the Word of God had been our guide, there would have been no retreat.

5. *Recover the spiritual disciplines for holy living.* Those disciplines include serious Bible study, intercessory prayer, systematic tithing, sacrificial fasting and daily solitude. While recognizing that these disciplines alone will not produce a holy life, we also know that we cannot be holy without them. Especially in the unlaxity of our age, expressed openly on the campus, a person who is maturing in personal and social holiness stands out as a witness to the faith. Yet this may be the point that troubles us most. We are quick to excuse ourselves because we don't want to come off as "holier than thou"

among our peers. But, in truth, that is the least of our problems today. Small souls do not lead to Great Awakenings. Spiritual discipline is time-consuming, ego-shaking and comfort-crushing. Elton Trueblood says it for us, "One cannot give what one does not have."[7]

6. *Keep a personal journal of spiritual growth.* Some of the richest reading in Christian history is the journals of believers who have recorded an account of their spiritual journey. Augustine's *Confessions,* for instance, are unparalleled for their psychological insights and Wesley's *Journal* is a spiritual adventure in itself. Although our journals may not become classic reading for future generations, they serve as checkpoints for our spiritual journey. Having kept a journal since 1966 in which I try to record almost every day some spiritual insight, test of faith, point of failure, spurt of growth, or answered prayer, I find an occasional reading of those daybooks a time for rejoicing, praising God and pledging myself to trust him more. Although many of the entries are confidential, there are times when I share them with my family, friends and confidants. Likewise, there are times when they share their journal entries with me and others. The insights invariably contribute to mutual edification.

7. *Maintain the link with the church.* We cannot forget that the cycle of the Spirit which leads to a Great Awakening includes the renewal of the church. In each generation the young are impatient with the church's cumbersome machinery and stodgy tradition. That's why the vitality of campus cells is easily substituted for what is perceived to be the deadness of the denomination or the local church. That's why Great Awakenings produce parachurch ministries that respond to spiritual needs neglected by the institutional church. But there is another side to the story. As Howard Snyder points out in his book *Signs of the Spirit,* renewal movements grow out of "ecclesiola in ecclesia," or a little church within the church.[8] Cells groups on the campus should conceive of themselves as "ecclesiola" with a solemn responsibility for renewal in the "ecclesia."

As the Great Awakenings of the past have shown us, when God pours out his Spirit on all people, revivals on the campus providentially connect with revivals in the church and vice versa. Neither the campus cell nor the institutional church can ever assume that it has a "corner on the Spirit." Just as Joel prophesied a multi-generational outpouring of the Spirit on the young, the middle-aged and the old, we must also expect a multi-structural outpouring in a Great Awakening—on the cell, the church and parachurch organizations for the singular purpose of building up the whole body of Christ.

8. *Continuously share with others the spiritual vitality of the cell.* Perhaps it has been said several different ways by now, but cell groups are in constant danger of becoming in-grown. Lyle Schaller, who has studied the development of prayer and Bible study groups in churches, confirms this danger in fact as well as theory.[9] Either from preoccupation with the inner life or by lapsing into the comfort of old friends, the cell group can stagnate and become self-serving.

This tendency is magnified as cultural conflict and individual stress increase. Here's why. Surprisingly, media studies show that instantaneous and full-color coverage of world affairs does not necessarily increase viewers' global awareness. More likely, we retreat into the security of our parochialism because television shows us only the problems and leaves us with no solutions in which we can participate.

The same reversal can take place in campus cell groups. As the enormity of the task of world evangelism confronts us, the corruption of the culture repels us and the failures of our own spiritual journey frustrate us, we will be tempted to retreat into the security of the cell. This cannot be. In *Signs of the Spirit,* Howard Snyder writes,

> Renewal moves out like concentric ripples in a pond, reaching beyond the Christian community to the whole human community. Biblical Christians, in fact, will be satisfied with nothing less: personal renewal, which becomes church renewal, which reaches to social renewal, which sweeps on to become world renewal.[10]

If we are under the authority of the Word of God and obedient to the heavenly vision, the centrifugal force of the Spirit will throw us ever outward—*from* the cell, *to* the campus, *through* the church, *among* the poor and *away* to the ends of the earth!

7 | The Network: Instrument for Evangelism

An audience of several hundred college students is a welcome sight for me. There I am at home; there I come alive; there I love to minister. Recently, however, I saw my college congregation through new eyes.

As a speaker at a ministers' conference on a college campus, I had also been asked to address the student body in chapel. The theme for the conference was "The Inclusive Church—God's Forgotten People." Along with the ministers, I struggled futilely with the subject. Finally we confessed together that, despite all of our preaching and posturing, eleven o'clock on Sunday morning still represented the most segregated hour of the week for our congregations.

No one could dispute the good intentions of the ministers who were present. They had come to the conference with the high, perhaps desperate, hope of finding a solution to the "exclusive" character of their white, middle-class, Anglo-Saxon congregations. In my addresses I offered tons of theology and plenty of passion, but when it came down to practical helps for a "take-home" program, I had little to offer. So, in the midst of my frustration, I especially welcomed the opportunity to speak to college students.

One look at my chapel audience that morning and the Spirit opened my eyes. For the first time, I saw the vision of "The Inclusive Church." The students were no longer a blurred mass before me. Faces of different colors, cultures and classes all came into view. Then I remembered the clusters of students with whom I had met on the campus. Without exception, they represented a mix of abilities, affiliations and aspirations as well as a diversity of age, race, sex and ethnic origin. The New Testament vision of the body of Christ came into view. My mind caught fire and my heart leaped—I knew then why God had so often chosen to visit college students with his Spirit as the beginning of a Great Awakening. *Even in the smallest clusters of students on campus, God sees the microcosm of his inclusive church around the world!* The campus is the natural network for transmitting the spirit and the message of a Great Awakening.

Networking in the Great Awakenings

Long before "networking" was borrowed from the electronic media in the twentieth century, Christians had discovered its meaning in the revivals that led to the Great Awakenings. While we remember the Holy Club at Oxford in the eighteenth century as a special and single cell of Christian students, the Wesleyan historian Richard Paul Heitzenrater reports a "university network of cell groups, more or less following John Wesley's scheme" throughout England by the mid-1730s.[1]

The same phenomenon of networking developed in each of the Great Awakenings in American history. J. Edwin Orr, the historian of revival, reports the miraculous connections among such colleges as Harvard, William and Mary, the University of Pennsylvania, Princeton, Columbia, Queens, Rutgers, Dartmouth and Brown in the Great Awakening of the mid-1700s. Fifty years later when the Awakening of the 1790s began at Yale, the Spirit of God created another collegiate network of campus revival which expanded to include Amherst, Dartmouth, Williams and Princeton. Shortly after the turn of the century, then, the collegiate awakenings spread west where Christian colleges were founded by the score. In Ohio, for instance, revivals served as the incentive for the founding of such schools as Denison, Oberlin, Hiram, Kenyon, Ohio Wesleyan, Baldwin-Wallace, Heidelberg and Otterbein. William Warren Sweet writes:

No phase of the religious development of America has been more misunderstood and as a consequence more maligned than has revivalism. It has been the victim of much cheap debunking. . . . Strange as it may seem to those who think only of revivalism in terms of ignorance . . . *there is a very close relationship between the history of higher education in America and revivalism.*[2] (italics mine)

Move on to the Great Awakening of the mid-1800s. YMCA chapters on the campuses of the University of Pennsylvania and the University of Michigan formed yet another network of cell groups committed to revival and dedicated to evangelism. The magnitude of this network, however, pales against the 352 educational institutions in the United States and Canada which were represented at the first international convention of the Student Volunteer Movement at Cleveland in 1891. Twenty-five years later, at its peak, John Mott reported that the movement involved 40,000 students in 700 colleges!

With the passing of another fifty years, the evangelical Christian colleges surfaced as the catalytic force for campus awakening. As we have already noted, the Spirit visited those campuses separately and simultaneously in 1950 and 1970. As the word of campus revival spread, the colleges of Anderson, Asbury, Baylor, Bethel, Greenville, Spring Arbor, Seattle Pacific, Taylor and Wheaton discovered a common spirit and distinctive mission. History leaves little doubt. "Evangelical Christianity was one of the major forces in the development of higher education in America and, indeed, in the spread of education throughout the world."[3] With the same potential for strength and vitality, *the collegiate network of Christian students is a natural instrument for a Great Awakening.*

Understanding a Network

Networks are creatures of need. John Naisbitt in *Megatrends* foresees networks as an organizational feature of the future in the Age of Information. Hierarchies, he suggests, gain their power from privileged information. But as more and more information is made available to the masses, hierarchies will break down and networks will arise.[4] Especially in the field of religion, if denominational hierarchies fail to respond to changing human needs and rising moral concerns, networks will naturally arise. The charismatic movement is an example. When traditional denominational structures did not make room for charismatic expression, people found each other across the lines of Catholic and Protestant faiths, Calvinist and Arminian theologies, Anglican and Pentecostal denominations. Likewise, as we have already mentioned, Jerry Falwell created the Moral Majority out of groups of people across religious, social, economic and political lines. They were drawn together because no established hierarchy adequately addressed their common concern—morality in America and, especially, the right to life.

Networking is particularly appealing to college students for the same reason. A network serves a need to which the hierarchy does not respond. The phenomenon in the history of Great Awakenings arose out of spiritual needs unmet by the established church. Especially we remember the networks of the Great Awakenings which were created among the masses of common people. George Whitefield had his network of field preaching; Francis Asbury his camp-meetings; D. L. Moody, his city crusades; and John R. Mott, his campus missions movement. College students naturally respond to the vision and vigor of such ventures.

The nature of a network also helps us understand why it appeals to college students. By definition, a network:

☐ focuses on a single issue,
☐ engages the interest of the masses,

☐ welcomes a diversity of people,

☐ relies on open communication,

☐ equalizes power among the members,

☐ exists in dynamic and flexible connections,

☐ creates a sense of belonging among its members,

☐ thrives on changing circumstances, and

☐ continues only as long as it is effective.

The match between the interests of the college student and the characteristics of a network is uncanny. Read again the definition of a network, but this time apply the characteristics to the way in which college students think and work. The nature of the network and the interests of a college student are almost synonymous. No wonder networks have arisen naturally as instruments of Great Awakenings.

Creating a Network

Three conditions are necessary for the creation of a network. First, there must be *ambiguity* about a moral issue. Second, there must be *diverse masses* of people who are concerned about the issue but find no solution in traditional organizations. Third, there must be *relevant information* available that addresses the issue and provides the basis for proposing a solution. The climate of the campus meets all of these expectations. Students, in their diversity, are trapped in the ambiguity of cultural conflict for which traditional institutions offer no answers. When the Spirit of God stirs them through a personal experience or a prophetic word, they respond and find each other, first in cells, and then in networks that can embrace the world.

At the 1989 Lausanne II Congress on World Evangelization held in Manila, we glimpsed the future of networking. While the Lausanne Committee remained intact and several organizations vied for identity as leaders in evangelizing the globe by A.D. 2000, the real action took place around dining tables, in lobbies and at seminars designed for special-interest tracks. In these settings people and ministries found each other, shared ideas, exchanged cards and promised to remain in contact after the conference closed. Soon I found myself

working the Congress on a networking strategy:
1. Meet as many people as I can;
2. Find the natural connection of our interests;
3. Cultivate the personal relationship;
4. Explore the potential for cooperation in ministry;
5. Agree to keep in communication after the Congress.

When I returned home and made a checklist of my contacts, I found myself humming, "He's Got the Whole World in His Hands." In one way or another I had made connections with people on every continent and with ministries of every type. For the first time my vision for world evangelization became feasible.

Backing up that vision, technology is a special friend of networking. At Lausanne II we met Christian scholars from behind what was then the Iron Curtain who were desperate for communication and interaction with other scholars in their fields. Another large group of educators came from the Two-Thirds World, where they did research and teaching with the most minimal of scholarly resources. When we asked, "How can we help meet their needs?" the idea of INTERNET came forward. Computer technology is now available at manageable cost to create a global network that can identify Christian scholars by field and permit them to communicate with each other by electronic mail and computer bulletin board. For the first time in history we have the opportunity to create a global network of Christian scholarships in support of world evangelism. One hundred years ago John R. Mott had the vision and the passion for "evangelizing the world in our generation." Today we have the practices—not just global communication systems but multiple ministries that literally embrace the world. After Lausanne II, I see the world suspended in a net of interconnected ministries that will leave no corner untouched and no spiritual need unmet. Networking is the instrument for the coming Great Awakening. Perhaps as never before, the college campus in the 1990s is a microcosm of the world. *With college students as networkers by nature and with the Spirit of God leading the way, we already have the global connections for a Great Awakening.*

8 | *The Leader: Agent of Hope*

Great Awakenings need prophetic leaders. The names of those leaders in the Great Awakenings in American history read like an addendum to the honor roll of the heroes of the faith in the Epistle to the Hebrews: Jonathan Edwards, George Whitefield, Timothy Dwight, Peter Cartwright, Francis Asbury, Charles Finney, Phoebe Palmer, Richard Allen, D. L. Moody, E. Stanley Jones, John R. Mott and others.

At the same time, no Great Awakening either began with or centered in a single personality. Rather we remember the Awakenings as grassroots movements, arising out of small cell groups and spreading spontaneously to the masses through the impulses of the awakening Spirit. Personality cults, to which we are prone today, contradict God's purpose for a spiritual awakening that reaches the masses, renews the church and reforms the culture. Prophetic leaders play an essential role in the cycle of the Spirit, but they are never on center stage throughout the drama. Instead, they make their entrance and their exit under the prompting of the Spirit. Still, whatever their role, they share some qualities of leadership which we must recover for the Great Awakening of the 1990s.

An Engaging Vision

Prophetic leaders need prophetic visions. When Daniel Burnham, the architect, envisioned building the great city of Chicago, he said, "Make no small dreams, for they have not magic to stir men's blood." His words might be paraphrased for the leaders of the Great Awakenings, "See no small vision, for it has no power to stir the soul." The test of our vision is whether or not we engage the excitement and commitment of others so thoroughly that our vision becomes their vision. After all, a leader is best defined as a person with followers. Until the vision of the leader and followers becomes one, there is no awakening. Nathan Hatch, in his book *The Democratization of American Christianity,* notes the common characteristics of leaders in the Great Awakenings of the nineteenth century:

> However diverse their theologies and church organizations, they all offered common people, especially the poor, *compelling visions of individual self-respect and collective self-confidence.*[1]
> (italics mine)

George Whitefield, a leader of the Great Awakening of the 1740s, drew criticism from the clergy when he went outside of the church to preach in the fields to the common people. He would have failed except for the momentum of the masses who followed him. Established, entrenched leaders of the institutional church always lose their case against visionaries who rally the masses by meeting their spiritual needs.

John R. Mott could have been accused of messianic hallucinations when he coined the watchword "To evangelize the world in our generation." But who can argue against the evidence of 40,000 college students who volunteered to march to that drumbeat for the rest of their lives? When Mott stood up and declared, "We can do it!" his followers believed him and then set off to make the watchword a reality. Did they reach their goal? If the current statistics on "unreached peoples" are accurate, it would appear as if they failed. Only the perspective of eternity can show us whether or not those students set in motion the witness that will win the world.

Still, the fact is that they gave themselves to the task and left us a legacy that keeps the watchword alive today in a new generation with the energized vision and the sophisticated technology to back it up. Who knows? *Today's world evangelism may be just a mop-up operation for the vanguard of youthful missionaries who saturated the globe a hundred years ago.*

A Meaningful Message

Leaders may have a vision that excites the imagination and engages the commitment of followers, but *they must be able to communicate that vision in day-to-day terms that are meaningful to those who follow.* In other words, prophetic voices in a Great Awakening must have the "power of democratic persuasion" to match their conviction that their message is the "pure fountain" of the faith. Keep in mind the special meaning of the prophetic voice. It is neither the standard sound heard in the institutional church that fails to address the changing needs of people, nor is it the nativist sound that harks back to traditional values alone. Rather, *the prophetic voice of a leader in a Great Awakening sounds the fresh note of the rediscovery of the gospel which is both true to the eternal Word and relevant to the changing world.*

We can trace the evolving nature of the prophetic voice in the histories of the Great Awakenings in America. Without passing judgment on the theological implications, *the issue of free will versus determinism has been at stake in each Awakening.* Jonathan Edwards broke from old-line Calvinism with his insistence upon personal repentance and public confession of faith as an act of will for his parishioners. For the colonists struggling for self-determination, he struck a prophetic chord for a political revolution as well as a spiritual awakening. Francis Asbury and Peter Cartwright took the act of free will in salvation a step farther. With their Methodist camp-meeting theology, they offered "free grace in all; free grace for all" by repentance at a mourner's bench. Despite opposition, their prophetic note struck a responsive chord on the egalitarian frontier and helped confirm our democracy.

Charles Finney took the issue of free will still another step when he dared to claim that revivals came by the faithfulness of Christians in intercessory prayer and good planning rather than waiting for a spontaneous and miraculous outpouring of God's Spirit.

Still later in the century liberal theologians took the question full cycle when they abandoned the supernatural and personal meaning of redemption in favor of human efforts in the Social Gospel. Those who remained true to the faith, however, sought to balance the sovereignty of God with the freedom of human will. As part of the Student Volunteer Movement at the turn of the century, William Borden of Yale represents the obedience to divine will when he made a free, lifetime choice for world missions with the declaration "No reserve, no retreat, no regrets."[2]

Earlier, when we outlined the cycle of the Spirit, we also noted that the rediscovery of the gospel for the prophetic voice may be personal or conceptual. Again, without passing theological judgment, we have seen examples of personal and conceptual rediscovery in recent years. The charismatic movement represents the rediscovery of the gospel as a personal experience. Millions have responded to the prophetic voices of evangelical preachers who promise the confirmation of holiness by the gifts of the Spirit. At the other extreme liberation theologians have rediscovered the gospel conceptually by wedding Marxist ideology and Christian theology as a response to the needs of oppressed people in Central and South America. Right or wrong, we cannot deny the prophetic nature of these voices and the impact they have had on the masses.

George Gallup, Jr., in *The People's Religion: America's Faith in the 1990s,* informs us that the first need of people today is to have faith communicated in terms that are meaningful to their lives.[3] Young persons, in particular, will make the choice of church on this basis.

The message is clear and crisp. Whoever communicates faith in meaningful terms, whether Christianity or cult, will win both the young and the masses.

Who will lead with the prophetic voice for the cause of Christ in the Great Awakening of the 1990s? The question awaits an answer.

A Tested Integrity

One of the most gratifying observations from the survey of Great Awakenings is the absence of scandal among the leaders. Certainly they were not exempt from the most severe criticism: Jonathan Edwards lost his pulpit; George Whitefield reaped ostracism from the clergy; Francis Asbury got stung with the label of an empty-headed oaf; D. L. Moody suffered the stigma of his enigmatic style; and E. Stanley Jones lived with the accusation of compromise because he contextualized the gospel for the people of India.

Criticism, however, is not scandal. While the leaders in the Great Awakenings may have escaped the scrutiny of television's eye, the consistency of their lives gave their message its integrity. They, like the apostle Paul, preached only what they themselves had experienced (Rom 15:18). We also remember that the leaders in past Awakenings came to leadership out of a cell group where they learned *spiritual discipline* and *mutual accountability.* Other than the experience of redemption itself, no two learning experiences are more important in the development of spiritual leaders. Here is where cell groups for students on the college campus play such a crucial role in preparing leaders for awakening.

Spiritual discipline protects the soul from contamination; mutual accountability saves the ego from arrogance. A friend who is a management consultant watched televangelists rise in power. After visiting with some of them and studying their organizations, he predicted, "They are in for trouble because they have no one around them to tell them no."

Billy Graham is one of the exceptions. Like many leaders in spiritual awakenings who preceded him, Graham's ministries have been scandal-free for almost fifty years, even though his life has been under microscopic scrutiny. Years ago, in the book *Up the Organization,* Robert Townsend used crude language to commend Billy Graham for gathering around him a team of people who can tell him no. Mutual accountability as a complement to spiritual discipline may be why Billy Graham's integrity backs up his anointing.

When Billy Graham opened the Kingdome Stadium in Seattle, Washington, in 1976 with a ten-day crusade, he held his usual press conference before the meetings began. As a skeptical group of reporters grilled him, a religion writer for a local newspaper launched a personal attack on Graham. The man, his motive and his ministry all came under caustic fire.

Later in the day I picked up Mrs. Graham to speak to the students at Seattle Pacific University where I served as president. On the way to the campus she told me, "I've never seen Billy so depressed. He feels as if he failed in this morning's press conference, especially with the religion editor who attacked him."

Still later that afternoon I happened to meet a graduate of the university, who covered social issues for the same newspaper as the religion editor who had mounted the attack. Not knowing of my conversation with Mrs. Graham, she told how she arrived at the desk in the city room to find her colleague tearing out sheet after sheet from his typewriter and throwing them on the floor in a clutter. Finally, he turned to her and spoke with frustration, "Billy Graham is hard to attack. The man is genuine." When his story appeared in next morning's newspaper, he concluded his mixed review with the same words, "Whatever else might be said, Billy Graham is genuine."

In the search for leaders in the Great Awakening of the 1990s, integrity is the first and last qualification. It is first because Christian leaders claim no integrity of their own outside of redeeming grace; it is last because more often than not, personal integrity is the witness that the world expects and critics cannot deny. No better training ground for integrity exists than in the cell group of the campus. College students can be brutally honest and gently forgiving. To learn

the pattern of spiritual discipline and the practice of mutual accountability during the college career is the best preparation for leaders
in the coming Great Awakening.

A Personal Sacrifice

Leaders empower their people through their own self-sacrifice. Francis
Asbury is a case in point. He is an exception among the leaders of
the Great Awakenings because he retained an episcopal structure and
an authoritarian style in American Methodism rather than following
the path of others toward a more democratic pattern. Yet, through
that episcopal structure and authoritarian style, he gave himself so
thoroughly to his people that thousands of young men responded to
his call for circuit-riders who were willing to give their life away.
Moreover, he gave himself so thoroughly to the common people on
the Western frontier that the momentum continued even after his
death in 1816 so that Methodism doubled in the decade between
1820 and 1830!

> Asbury's life is a heroic testament. . . . [He] introduced Method-
> ism to thousands of young itinerants during his thirty-one years
> as a bishop. Yet he never asked a preacher to endure a hardship
> that he did not undertake regularly. . . . He never found time to
> marry, build a home, or to accumulate possessions beyond what
> a horse could carry. He shared the same subsistence allotment
> from the churches as any Methodist itinerant. . . . [His] circuit
> averaged five thousand miles annually and took him across the
> Alleghenies sixty-two different times. He preached daily, slept in
> the crudest of hovels, maintained a massive correspondence and
> was responsible for the entire army of itinerants—some seven
> hundred strong at the time of his death.[4]

When Asbury left the comfort of the Eastern cities for the hazards of
the wilderness, he told his clerical colleagues who preferred to stay
behind, "I'll show you the way." He did and left us the legacy of
leadership in the spirit of Christ: "unless a kernel of wheat falls to
the ground and dies, it remains only a single seed. But if it dies, it

produces many seeds" (Jn 12:24). Prophetic voices that speak without self-sacrifice fall on deaf ears.

A Creative Genius

I intentionally left to last the quality of genius that characterized the prophetic leaders of the Great Awakenings. It is also least. Without the prior qualities of personal integrity and self-sacrifice, genius in religious leaders becomes self-serving and self-glorifying. *Yet we cannot ignore or deny the creativity required to communicate the gospel on some frontier among the masses,* which is always a part of a Great Awakening. Whether it is Asbury's army of circuit-riders or Finney's strategic planning for city crusades, Nathan Hatch is right when he notes that the leaders of the Great Awakenings in the nineteenth century were tireless workers, idealistic dreamers, systematic planners and, in some cases, religious mavericks.[5]

In our day, the test of innovative techniques and entrepreneurial methods necessarily involves the use of media in communicating the gospel. A few years ago I had the privilege of being the guest of the late Gordon Rupp for high tea in the Great Hall at Cambridge University, which overlooks the courtyard where the race in *Chariots of Fire* was filmed. Professor Rupp was recognized as the premier historian of the Wesleyan revival in England during the eighteenth century. I was on sabbatical at Cambridge to study primary sources of Wesleyan history to see if I could discover the genius of John Wesley's leadership.

While probing the mind of Professor Rupp, I took the risk of asking him the kind of question that historians inevitably avoid: "Dr. Rupp, if John Wesley were alive today, would he be on television?" Without the slightest hesitation, he answered in his crisp British accent, "Unquestionably!"

Nathan Hatch notes that the use of media as a means for communicating the gospel to the masses is dominated by Pentecostals and fundamentalists in our generation.[6] A few of them have almost spoiled it, but most of us have missed it. *In the Great Awakening of*

*the 1990s the media will have to be recovered by young leaders who
are credible as well as creative.*

When the apostles appointed deacons for the New Testament
church, they set the criteria: persons of good report, practical wisdom
and the infilling of the Holy Spirit (Acts 6:1-7). Whether in the first
century or the twenty-first century, these criteria still hold. Particularly
with the scandals, defections and breakdown of Christian leaders in
the 1980s, persons who qualify as leaders in the Great Awakening of
the 1990s must have the reputation of integrity before the world,
wisdom that is meaningful to the masses and the indwelling Spirit,
whose outpouring gives a vision big enough to stir the blood. The
call is out, especially to potential prophets on the college campus.
Who will lead us in the Great Awakening of the 1990s?

9 | *The Church: Body for Renewal*

*T*he church, along with our society's other primary institutions, is in trouble. Both its authority and its influence in the culture have been reduced by secularism on the outside, confusion on the inside and scandal at the top. An air of quiet desperation prevails:

☐ Roman Catholic bishops engage a multimillion-dollar public relations consultant to change the minds of its members on birth control and abortion;

☐ Mainline churches—Methodist, Presbyterian and Episcopal—suffer malaise from declining membership;

☐ The Southern Baptist Convention is paralyzed by a "holy war" between factions;

☐ Independent churches, usually centered in a pastoral personality, constitute the fastest-growing segment of religious institutions;

☐ The largest, fastest-growing local churches use market techniques to appeal to the "consumerism" of churchgoers;

☐ The National Council of Churches, dedicated to organic union, is torn apart by infighting;

☐ Evangelicals find themselves out of the center of power with a change of presidents.

These fragments verify that the church is in need of renewal, not just for its own sake but for the culture it is called to penetrate with the gospel.

The Masses in the Middle

Studs Terkel, after interviewing people across the nation, chose the title *The Great Divide* for a book to summarize his findings. Terkel describes Americans today as people who are divided over religion, with a gaping chasm between factions. On one side are conservatives, who join together in opposition to abortion, pornography and family breakdown but are hopelessly fragmented by independent churches and personality cults. On the other side are liberals, who find common ground on the issues of feminism, abortion rights and environmentalism but are equally fragmented despite ecumenical efforts. These two groups are at war, according to Terkel, lobbing missiles against each other over the wide chasm that divides them. In the middle are the masses, struggling with the moral dilemmas of life and death and receiving no adequate answers from either side.[1] The masses in the middle of the Great Divide send the strongest signal that the church needs a Great Awakening. As we have seen from the Great Awakenings of the past, it is the masses in the middle whose spiritual needs are met when the church is renewed.

Gaps in the Church

Our individualistic culture has weakened the church just at the time when it needs to be strong. With the rise of radical self-interest comes the decline of loyalty to any institution. In its place a consumer attitude develops, which always asks, "What's in it for me?" George Gallup, Jr., reports on America's religious consumerism:

They have a clear sense of what they want from their churches—

and, in fact, they tend to view their churches less as sources of faith than as resources for their personal and family religious and spiritual needs.[2]

College students especially demonstrate the loss of loyalty by the churches they choose. Denominational backgrounds and theological differences are becoming less and less important factors on which the choice of a church is made. Instead, like shoppers in a supermarket, they look on the items which are best displayed and most satisfying. The labels on the items, even the warning labels, either are not read or do not count. When college students choose churches this way, more often than not, no church satisfies. Private piety is the result. When one young woman was asked, "To which church do you belong?" she answered, "I am my own church." George Gallup, Jr., predicts that her attitude will be a major challenge to the church in the 1990s. Again Gallup reports, "While Americans value church membership and religious activity, they do not believe that formal institutional ties are necessary to faith."[3]

Still more crucial is the evidence of serious gaps in America's religious faith which profoundly affect the young:

☐ The "Ethics Gap" between religious belief and practice;

☐ The "Knowledge Gap" between spiritual experience and understanding; and

☐ The "Belonging Gap" between believers and congregational participation.[4]

For this reason the church needs renewal to answer the questions that are being asked by young people today. Their questions are essentially spiritual: How can I know God? How can I be saved? How can I face my own death?

What Will Happen?

In past Great Awakenings, as we have seen, either the existing institutional church was renewed or new ministries arose to answer these questions and serve the needs they represent. If current trends continue, it appears as if the church of the 1990s will move in one of three directions. First, *the local church may flourish again* as the population ages and young parents return to church for the sake of their children. Second, *special networks of ministries may grow* in response to specific needs among the masses—for example, single parenting, care for senior citizens, handicaps and many kinds of addiction counseling. A United Methodist pastor in Memphis, for instance, appeared in national religious news when he advertised a singles' church service for Sunday morning. Although he expected a handful of singles in response, more than 150 persons showed up. By surprise, the pastor had uncovered a current and future need.

Third, *the coming generation may drop out of church altogether* while keeping its religious identity in some form of private piety short of Christian maturity. At present, young adults under the age of twenty-five represent the largest group of unaffiliated believers. Gallup's predictions for the future of the church in the 1990s depend on whether or not these young adults choose to participate in local congregations when they reach their mid-twenties. As it is now, they are not returning to church until their mid-thirties or early forties. As Andrew Greeley has found in his study entitled *Religious Change in America,* "baby boomers" of the 1950s and 1960s are now returning to church for the sake of their children. The good news is that these baby boomers recognize the need for their children to have the religious nurture of the church. The bad news is that they cannot provide the base for that nurture out of their own experience. Greeley notes that the baby-boomer parents represent the first generation in American history without Scripture in their heads, a hymn in their hearts or a memory of prayer in their homes.[5] Baby boomers, despite their education, affluence and sophistication, are like their children—neophytes in the faith.

Urgency intensifies the need for renewal. Unless the church responds to the needs of the masses in the middle, ecstatic Eastern and cultic religions will meet those needs. John Naisbitt, in *Megatrends 2000,* believes that the gap is already being filled by two kinds of religious responses. One is a form of fundamentalism that takes the

Bible so literally that it has "cash register" authority for the questions of life and death. No other authority, except experience, is allowed. Reason and tradition are definitely rejected and even Jesus' promise that the Holy Spirit will lead us into all truth is suspect.

Signs of this trend are evidenced on the college campus, where some students are reading Frank Peretti's *Piercing the Darkness* and *This Present Darkness* as if the novels were a new revelation. To hear fiction quoted like a biblical prooftext and hear demonic or angelic explanations for every happening in life, with exorcism as the solution, is a distortion of both truth and fiction. If college students read Peretti as gospel truth, one can only imagine the impact on the masses who are uneducated, impoverished and out of power. A spiritual point of control outside themselves offers the explanation and gives them the security that they need.

New Age religion is the other extreme that is filling the gap and answering the questions for the masses in the middle.[6] Although Naisbitt is biased as a New Age believer himself, his findings cannot be dismissed out of hand. In effect, the New Age movement is the old human potential movement flying its full colors. Totally naturalistic, humanistic and pantheistic, the New Age takes root in radical self-interest turned theological. Steeped in the faith that "we are gods" the New Age movement locates the source of truth within the inherent goodness and incipient godliness of human nature. Here is the appeal to the young, educated, affluent and professional members of the masses in the middle. Without adequate grounding in Scripture, hymns and prayer from their homes, they are the ready targets of cults.

Great Awakenings have the distinction of addressing the needs of both educated and uneducated people. What better example can we cite than the Great Awakening that began in the 1790s on the Gothic campus of Yale and extended in the early 1800s to the sawdust trail of a frontier camp meeting? Or remember that Francis Asbury, an unlearned man, founded a school that later became a Christian liberal arts college? Out of that two-pronged movement came the renewal of the church as it stretched to serve both the classes and the masses.

The need will intensify in the 1990s. George Gallup, Jr., presents evidence in *The People's Religion* to predict that in the coming decade, the American people will be "less Protestant, less Western, less white, but more Catholic, more Mormon and more unaffiliated."[7]

Gallup's prediction is based on two factors that he considers crucial to the future of denominations. One is the ability of the denomination to bring its youth into membership; the other is the effectiveness of the denomination in evangelistic outreach. These two factors expose the faultlines of mainline denominations which are failing to retain their youth or win new members. The same two factors tell us why Mormons are predicted to be among the fastest-growing denominations and why evangelicals can continue to increase in numbers if our emphasis on youth and evangelism is continued.

Add still another note of threat and opportunity for the institutional church and our denominations. *Time* magazine for April 9, 1990, featured an article entitled "Beyond the Melting Pot." Following population and racial trends into the twenty-first century, *Time* concludes: "In the lifetime of our babies, if current trends continue, white Anglo-Saxons will be a minority in America."[8]

This prediction is based on the fact that Hispanic, Asian and African peoples are doubling in numbers while European descendants are in steady state. If the trends continue, by 2056 the "average American" will not be a white person of European ancestry but a brown, yellow or black person of Hispanic, Asian or African ancestry. Consequently, we can expect the Roman Catholic Church to grow as the Hispanic population grows and world religions such as Buddhism and Islam to become a force in the future as Asian, Middle Eastern and African immigrants increase. If the Christian church has ever faced a challenge for the future, this is it.

A radical adjustment is needed. Rather than assuming that church growth comes from evangelizing homogeneous types of people who are compatible with the congregation and ready for the gospel, a

Great Awakening will require a church that answers the spiritual questions all people are asking, responds to "the browning of America," and creates new forms of ministry on the fast-developing racial and religious frontiers of the 1990s.

For these reasons alone, we cannot limit revival to the college campus. While Christian college students are best equipped to meet the needs of ethnic peoples on the new frontier, they, filled by the outpouring of God's Spirit, must take their vision for the "masses in the middle," the "classes at the top" and the "ethnics on the edges" to their local churches and give themselves in ministry to one or more of these diverse needs. *Without this vision for the church, there will be no renewal.*

10 | *The Culture: Field for Reform*

*I*n *a Great Awakening, revival among the masses leads to renewal* in the church that, in turn, opens the way for reform in the culture. The fundamental point must be pressed home again: *Without reform in the culture there is no Great Awakening.*

Freedom is most often the issue on which Great Awakenings turn. In the eighteenth century, the issue was *political freedom* from the oppression of England. In the nineteenth century, the nation divided over *social freedom* for the slaves. Is freedom still the issue today? If so, what is the kind of freedom for which we need a Great Awakening in the 1990s?

Sorting Out the Issues

Looking back on history, it is easy to oversimplify issues. Our perspective on the Great Awakenings of the past helps us see the turning points of political freedom in the eighteenth century and social freedom in the nineteenth century. But if we were alive at the time, the moral complexity of those issues would undoubtedly overwhelm us. Or today, if we read the works of historians of those times, the tangled web of interrelated factors confound us. Politics, economics, geography, sociology, history, philosophy and even theology of the times are inseparably entwined.

Yet, those of us who are convinced that the issues of our day especially reflect the intrusion of secular humanism need to read *Faith of Our Fathers* by Edwin S. Gaustad. With the insight of an historian who has lived with primary sources, he writes that the public at large in 1789 reacted against the Constitution because it "failed to make religious liberty secure" and, worse yet, "failed to honor the dominant faith of the people."[1] His concluding observation gives us a perspective on the issues of those times—and ours: "Neither dunces nor idlers could do much about dangers and dragons in those days, nor—one suspects—in our own."[2]

Diligence, then, is required of us as we reflect on the issues of our times and sort them out for priority in a Great Awakening. Certainly we feel as if the complexity of the past has increased in the twentieth century. Political, social, economic, moral and spiritual issues are compounded by an interdependent world subjected to instantaneous communications, technological advancement and bureaucratic build-up. Whatever else we may think about instantaneous and global communications, the media have made us more aware of the issues which confront us. In fact, the issues of the 1990s are already sorting themselves out. John Naisbitt in *Megatrends 2000* puts priority on the trends which he has observed in the news items of the five "flagship" states that he continuously monitors:[3]

1. The Booming Global Economy of the 1990s
2. A Renaissance in the Arts
3. The Emergence of Free Market Socialism
4. Global Lifestyles and Cultural Nationalism
5. The Privatization of the Welfare State
6. The Rise of the Pacific Rim
7. The Decade of Women in Leadership

8. The Age of Biology

9. The Religious Revival of the New Millennium

10. The Triumph of the Individual

In this listing of trends Naisbitt again exposes the faultline of his thinking—the error of his New Age mentality. With just a nod of the head toward the human hurts of poverty, illness, divorce, abuse, drugs, illiteracy and crime, he leaves the bad news to other prognosticators. A litany of these social ills is not necessary. We know that Naisbitt's evolving human consciousness cannot leave in its wake the impoverished and the disenfranchised with only the promise that a rising tide of human consciousness raises all ships. *Human conscience must rise with human consciousness or disaster is inevitable.*

Perhaps with a prophetic twist, theologians and sociologists are also scanning the religious landscape to develop a working agenda for the 1990s and the third millennium. Hans Küng, the controversial Roman Catholic theologian, has written a book entitled *Theology for the Third Millennium* in which he views the present-day crisis in terms of losses. His list includes the *loss of confidence* in science and technology, education and intellect, church and theology; the *loss of credibility* for Western dominance and Christian superiority; and the *loss of support* for racist and sexist systems.[4]

Against this bleak picture, Küng sees the renewal of the church for the third millennium in a new theological paradigm (a word meaning "pattern," which theologians use as easily as teen-agers say, "You know"). The new paradigm, according to Küng, sets the theological agenda for the church in the twenty-first century to resolve the tension between:

☐ the Roman Catholic view of authority in the tradition of the church and the Protestant view of authority in the revelation and the Word;

☐ the traditional view of history, which is true to past learning, and the contemporary view of history, which is relevant to present reality;

☐ the Christocentric view of salvation, which makes Christ the

only Savior, and the ecumenical view of salvation, which finds
hope for redemption in world religions;

☐ the scholarly view of truth, which sees it as relative, and the
pastoral view of truth, which holds truth as absolute.[5]

As you might guess, these tensions are so extreme that Küng can only
resolve them by compromising the revelation of the Word, the pre-
cepts of history, the redemption of Christ and the authority of absolute Truth. Still, in his new paradigm, he dares to confront the issues
that we cannot afford to avoid.

John Stott, one of evangelical Christianity's most respected theologians, takes another approach to the issues of the future in his
published symposium *The Year 2000.*[6] He foresees a series of on-
going debates over human rights, the arms race, economic compe-
tition, energy and environment, technological advancement and political freedom as the agenda for evangelical Christians in the next
decade.

Closer to home, George Gallup, Jr., surveyed more than one thousand opinion leaders in America to find out what they considered the
most serious problems facing us today. The issues that surfaced with
new urgency were: the nuclear threat, including terrorism; economic
weakness, including unemployment and its related symptoms of
crime and racial tension; and the health crisis, including substance
abuse and environmental poisons.[7]

More than the identification of issues is needed to reform the
culture. Küng, Stott and Gallup each call for a new paradigm or
conceptual repackaging on which to rebuild the moral consensus for
reform. In terms of the cycle of the Spirit I have outlined this would
fall under "Rediscovery of the Gospel."

Two problems, however, confront us when we depend on a new
paradigm as the basis for cultural transformation. One is the position
we have taken that *cultural transformation begins with personal
transformation.* The bankruptcy of the Social Gospel in this century
is all of the evidence we need. Two world wars and the Jewish
Holocaust are all the facts we need to rest our case. Yesterday's

advocates of the Social Gospel are today's neo-conservatives, who are better defined as "liberals who got mugged by reality." Without transforming grace a conceptual change will be no more than an academic exercise or a utopian dream—both doomed to fail.

The second problem is *the risk of compromising biblical truth.* This can happen in the process of accommodating differing viewpoints. In his *Theology for the Third Millennium,* Küng seems to fall into this trap when he tries to merge salvation alone in Jesus Christ with the truth in world religions. He comes out with the conclusion:

> And in the end there will no longer be standing between the religions a figure that separates them, no more prophet or enlightened one, not Muhammad and not the Buddha. Indeed even Christ Jesus, whom Christians believe in, will no longer stand here as a figure of separation. But he, to whom Paul says, all powers (including death) are subjected, "subjects himself, then, to God" so that God *himself* (ho theos)—or however he may be called in the East—may truly be just in all things, but "everything to everyone."[8]

If a new paradigm compromises the character of Christ, it will lack the "certain sound" required for the prophetic voice.

James Davison Hunter, in his book *Evangelicalism: The Coming Generation,* sets his criteria for evangelical renewal and social reform. He calls for the "binding address," which fires the moral energy of its adherents to work for change, serves as a catechism that can be taught to oncoming generations, and becomes the standard for moral discipline of behavior in the culture. Anthropologists who have studied cultural renewal see "binding address" with its *internal discipline* as the alternative to an *external attack* of persecution, which will also bind a subculture together and reform the culture itself. They forget the other option—the promise of Pentecost:

> In the last days, God says, I will pour out my Spirit on all people. Your sons and daughters will prophesy, your young men will see visions, your old men will dream dreams. (Acts 2:17)

What then is the vision of the young around which we can create the "binding address" of a new paradigm for social reform? When historians look back on our century and see the evidence of a Great Awakening, *what will be the issue of freedom at the cutting edge of social reform?*

Although I have expressed fundamental disagreement with the veiled New Age theology of John Naisbitt in *Megatrends 2000,* I concur with his opening statement about the future: "The most exciting breakthroughs of the twenty-first century will occur not because of technology but because of an expanding concept of what it means to be human."[9]

My definition of humanity, however, must be informed by biblical revelation, the character of Christ and the mind of the Holy Spirit as he leads us into all truth. To be fully human is to be:

☐ created in the image of God;

☐ sinful by nature and guilty of sin;

☐ redeemed by the death and resurrection of Jesus Christ;

☐ valued as a gifted person with the potential for personal, social and spiritual maturity;

☐ related to other persons, groups, the larger community and the body of Christ;

☐ responsible for living, loving, serving and dying to the glory of God.

In this context, I revise Naisbitt's view of the future to read: The most exciting breakthroughs of the twenty-first century will occur not because of technology but because of an expanding concept of what it means to be fully human and fully free *in Christ.*

What then is the breakthrough in our century that will parallel the political and social freedoms gained by Great Awakenings of the past? I choose the freedom that philosophically alienates most of us and practicably affects all of us—economic freedom. *Economic freedom is the issue which can only be decided by the social transformation of a Great Awakening in the last decade of the twentieth century.*

We look back with justifiable pride on the social transformation of political freedom from England in the Great Awakening of the eighteenth century and social freedom from slavery in the Great Awakening of the nineteenth century. Now we must look forward to economic freedom for the poor as the proof of a Great Awakening in the twentieth century. Because of America's wealth, this is the basis on which future generations will judge us.

Economic freedom, in this case, is not restricted either to fiscal concerns, such as the federal budget, or to economic systems, such as capitalism or communism. I intend the biblical meaning of the word *economics*. The root word in the Greek is *oikonomos*, or the "management of the household." By this literal definition, economic freedom includes our trusteeship of our God-given resources. Both individually and corporately, we will be held accountable for our stewardship of people, money, space, time, knowledge and energy. None of these resources is ours to own, and all of them are ours to manage.

To date, Christians have been little help in rediscovering the gospel for the management of our household of God-given resources. Because free-market capitalism is consistent with religious freedom, we have been slow to criticize it. On the other hand, because communism is so blatantly atheistic, we have been quick to condemn it. Furthermore, anyone who suggests a mixing of Christian theology and economic theory to produce some form of Judeo-Christian socialism is immediately shunted into a liberal or communist camp. And, of course, no quarter is given when Christian theology is merged with Marxist theory to produce Liberation Theology. The stalemate is permanent.

Meanwhile the poor cry out for a word of hope. Their numbers multiply by the millions. In North America the irony of our affluence shows up in beggars embarrassing us on street corners and sleeping derelicts shaming us in garbage bags over iron grates. Worst of all, statistics show a "new poor" among us, not simple schizophrenics or self-satisfied hobos but children of single-parent families and broken homes, victims of unemployment and ignorance, and forgotten members of urban and rural ghettos. They are the residue of a public, private and political attitude that has widened the gap between the rich and the poor in a land of plenty.

The issue is moral; the answer is spiritual. Tired arguments about communism will not suffice; preachy pronouncements about a simple lifestyle will not do. The opening events of the 1990s in communist countries of the world leave no doubt: *Individual initiative in a free market with sufficient regulation on human greed is the economic system that will prevail.* But what about the poor? They will continue to chafe under the chains of poverty unless our economic attitudes are transformed by the biblical meaning of stewardship. We must:

☐ acknowledge that God has entrusted to us all of our resources: people, money, space, time, energy and knowledge;

☐ accept the responsibility God has given us to manage his whole household; and

☐ recognize that God will hold us accountable for the use and investment of all his resources in his household.

If these principles are applied to the moral issues of the 1990s, our agenda for economic freedom comes clear. We must accept responsibility to:

☐ assure the sanctity of human life from conception to death;

☐ share our abundance with the poor at home and abroad;

☐ preserve the quality our physical and social environment;

☐ guarantee the economic, social and moral future of our families;

☐ require the ethical application of the ideas and inventions of human knowledge and

☐ conserve the irreplaceable sources of natural energy.

Because these issues of economic freedom are moral, it will take a Great Awakening on the campus, in the church and of the culture to transform our human greed into the most elementary principles of biblical stewardship. Such a transformation is possible—as we know from the Great Awakening that ran from the 1840s into the 1870s, based on policies of justice for Blacks, children and women, and complemented by the compassion of volunteers in nonprofit human service agencies. To foresee our nation sharing its abundance with the impoverished of the earth through an enlightened foreign policy, eliminating poverty at home through a shift in national priorities and assuring the future of our children by managing the national debt is not fiction. If a Great Awakening again sensitized the public conscience to the needs of the poor, our generation would be remembered with the same justifiable pride with which we look back on our political freedom from England and our social freedom for the slaves.

Whether or not such a new paradigm with "binding address" can be forged for the future depends on Christian students in the college setting who sense the urgency of the task. This urgency was expressed by Elton Trueblood, who said, "It is the vocation of Christians in every generation to outthink all opposition."[10] Charles Malik spoke with equal eloquence when he called Christian students to two tasks: "that of saving the soul and that of saving the mind."[11]

Beginning with personal redemption, the Christian student must take up the conceptual challenge of rethinking the truth for a changing age and forging that truth in the social, political, economic and religious crucibles of the culture. A Third Force of prophetic voices is needed. Between the First Force of the clergy who preach the gospel and the Second Force of the laity who live the gospel, the Third Force is leadership of Christians who penetrate the culture in every profession and offer Truth with prophetic hope for moral issues and human needs.

While the Third Force may begin on the campus, we cannot forget the point of penetration for the Great Awakenings of the past. Nathan Hatch reminds us that our predecessors in prophetic leadership were "remarkably effective in forging moral communities among the poor, the sick, the ignorant and the elderly—those most vulnerable in a rapidly industrializing society."[12] If he is right, the coming Great Awakening of the 1990s will also be guided by the reality of economic freedom for the least of those among us.

11 | *Anticipating the Great Awakening*

Human beings are creatures of anticipation. With hope, we live; without hope, we die. This is the impulse that helps us understand why the 1990s are so significant. We are in the last decade of the twentieth century and on the threshold of the third millennium. *Something exciting has to happen.* A quick scan of current bookshelves demonstrates a market already flooded with titles that capitalize on the theme of A.D. 2000:

- ☐ *Megatrends 2000*—John Naisbitt and Patricia Aburdene
- ☐ *Theology for the Third Millennium*—Hans Küng
- ☐ *Forecast 2000*—George Gallup, Jr.
- ☐ *The Year 2000*—John Stott
- ☐ *The Humane Imperative: A Challenge for the Year 2000*—Theodore Hesburgh
- ☐ *Religion in the Year 2000*—Andrew Greeley
- ☐ *Recreating Our Schools for the 21st Century*—James Lewis
- ☐ *The 2025 Report: A Concise History of the Future*—Norman Macrae

Complementing these intriguing titles is the growing bulk of newsprint given to the coverage of the year 2000. John Naisbitt, in *Megatrends 2000,* reports on the results of his clippings from newspapers in the five bellwether states that he constantly monitors: California, Florida, Washington, Colorado and Connecticut. He observes that an air of anticipation is rising in the 1990s toward the new millennium. This is not unusual. Throughout human history, the last decade before a new century and especially before a new millennium has been filled with apocalyptic hope and fear. One thousand years ago, for instance, people who lived in the decade of A.D. 990 envisioned the Second Coming of Christ and the beginning of the biblical millennium in A.D. 1000.

As we observed in chapter nine, Naisbitt believes that the early signs of a spiritual awakening in the 1990s are already with us. Again, unfortunately, he observes people responding to this spiritual renaissance in one of two extremes: ultra-fundamentalism or the New Age beliefs. So, while I agree with Naisbitt's reading of the signs of spiritual awakening in the 1990s, I cannot agree with his limited perception of the options. Our hope is not in theological excesses of ultra-fundamentalism or the humanistic extremes of the New Age movement but in the supernatural outpouring of the Spirit of God on all people.

Winds of Awakening

As we noted in the beginning of this book, there is evidence of the stirring of the Spirit in every corner of the globe. In the Two-Thirds World, Great Awakenings are already under way. Mass conversions of thousands of people are commonplace in Africa, Latin America and Southeast Asia. Not without significance, most of the people among those thousands are young. When the Spirit moves on them, they see visions of the future that remind us of the leaders of the Great Awakenings who "pursued people wherever they could be found; embraced them without regard for social standing; and challenged them to think, to interpret Scripture, and to organize the church for themselves."[1]

If the outpouring of the Spirit is preceded by the gusty winds of freedom, we must also recognize his stirring among *Communist* nations in Eastern Europe and China. Etched into our memory is the scene of students from East Germany chipping away at the Berlin Wall and singing, "This is the day that the Lord has made. We will rejoice and be glad in it." Story after story coming out of Eastern Europe confirm the fact that the drive for political freedom had its genesis in Christian students who were spiritually free.

As a frequent guest on college campuses, I am convinced that the Spirit is also stirring among *Christian students in North America.* Each time I talk about the "golden chain" of cell groups—the Holy Club, the Haystack Prayer Meeting, the YMCA and the twentieth-century prayer bands—someone informs me of such a group meeting on the campus at the present time. Furthermore, I cannot forget the most recent image of one thousand students standing in a college chapel to declare publicly their willingness to die to self and go wherever God may lead them. Their witness more than counters the dark side of campus life with its drug abuse, date rape, racial tension, lack of civility and loss of community. My son, a university senior, spoke for this generation of Christian students as he weighed his options—an MBA degree, law school or seminary—and concluded, "Dad, whatever I do, it must be ministry."

These stirrings of the Spirit remind us that God is full of surprises. Peter Kuzmic is the president of Evangelical Theological College in Osijek, Yugoslavia, an evangelical outpost in a communist country. At the World Congress on Evangelization in Manila in the summer of 1989, Peter spoke of his vision for educating Christian evangelists, pastors and teachers who would be ready to lead the church *if and when* the Iron Curtain crumbled in Eastern Europe. The vision seemed worthy but far off because of repressive action by the communist governments. Kuzmic had little idea how prophetic his message would be. Within four months the winds of freedom swept through the Eastern bloc of communist nations and opened the doors for the gospel.

In January 1990 Peter Kuzmic spoke again, this time to the Fellowship of Evangelical Seminary Presidents in the United States. When asked about the unpredicted, cataclysmic happenings in Eastern Europe, Peter answered, "Never put a period where God puts a comma!"

A week later David Seamands, professor of pastoral care at Asbury Theological Seminary, reinforced this lesson for me. In the last week of January I presented to our faculty a paper with the title "ATS—2000." My intention was to project the vision of ministry for Asbury in the next ten years. Dr. Seamands, a former missionary to India, read the paper and commented, "The title should be 'ATS—2001.' In India, we never fix the future on a round number because it means 'The End.' The year 2001, however, signifies an open future." How right he is. If we are alert to the stirrings of the Spirit among us, around us and beyond us, we will see the comma of God's promise rather than the period of our pessimism. This is not to deny the Second Coming of Christ or the end of time, but only to obey Christ's command, "What I say to you, I say to everyone: Watch!" (Mk 13:37). Peter Kuzmic's wise words should become our watchword for the coming Great Awakening, *"Never put a period where God puts a comma!"*

The Foundation for Awakening

To the stirrings of the Spirit among the students of the world, we must add the evidence that Americans have the elements of faith on which the cycle of Great Awakenings turns. Again, we are in for a surprise. George Gallup, Jr., in *The People's Religion: America's Faith in the 1990s,* reveals these facts about the *general public:*

☐ America's basic beliefs in God and the afterlife are as strong and stable in the 1980s and 1990s as they were in the 1930s and 1940s.

☐ Belief in Jesus Christ and commitment to him are even stronger now than in the 1970s.

☐ An increasing number of Americans are reading their Bibles daily.

☐ One-third of Americans, an increasing number, have experienced a personal and spiritual "moment of awakening."

Behind these facts are even more important findings regarding *young people* in America:

☐ While persons ages 18 to 24 are the least religious group in the nation, they will return to church on a life cycle in the mid-twenties when adult decisions are made and in the mid-thirties when children need the nurture of the church.

☐ College-age young people expect the church to give them meaning for their lives and emphasize spirituality in its ministry.

☐ The future growth of the church depends on the population under the age of 30 as the complement to evangelism.

☐ While young people under thirty intend to go to church more often in the next five years, the extent to which the church addresses their needs for meaning and spirituality will determine whether they will be among the adherents or the unaffiliated.

We can readily see that spiritually needy young people of college age represent the "turning point" for the church in the 1990s. The most crucial finding of all, however, may well be our legacy from Great Awakenings of the past: *College-educated youth in America do not reject religion.*

Our college educated youth stand in sharp contrast to the college-educated youth of Europe. In the nations of the European continent, existentialism is the "faith" of the young and the educated. For this reason, we can understand the spiritual bankruptcy of so many European nations and the despair for spiritual recovery. The college-educated youth of Europe not only espouse the philosophy of existentialism but they act it out in Marxist movements and self-destructive lifestyles.

Our college-educated youth may also be testing the extremes of radical self-interest on the campus, but when they do, they are rebelling against the foundations of their faith. As one college student told me, "Christian students on the campus may try wild things, but they cannot get away from their base." With our youth, as well as with the students of Europe, we must put a comma, not a period, on their spiritual state. Who knows? The Spirit may be stirring among the college-educated youth of Europe just as he is moving among college students in America. For us, the evidence that our college-educated youth do not reject religion is a most encouraging sign for the coming of a Great Awakening. If we can address their need for meaning in life and their thirst for spirituality in depth, they can bring the Great Awakening of the twentieth century full cycle in the revival of the masses, the renewal of the church and the reform of the culture.

Our New Frontier
In the Great Awakenings of the past, the young saw visions of new frontiers—George Whitefield, the fields of New England; Francis Asbury, the Western wilderness; D. L. Moody, the developing industrial cities; and John R. Mott, the nations of the world. Times have changed: our frontiers are no longer local; they are global. No longer can we think about a Great Awakening in American history as a local phenomenon of revival, renewal and reform. Rather, *we must see ourselves as part of a worldwide awakening*. In fact, we may be minor players with a late entrance into that global drama.

Look at the nations south of the equator. The Spirit is already being poured out on all flesh, and the young are seeing, not just visions of revival, renewal and reform for their nations, but a missiological vision for the world. To the shock of our American ego, we learn that the United States is sixteenth among the nations sending missionaries overseas![2] Although the adjustment is radical, we may need to turn upside-down our *sending/receiving* view of missions and to realize that we are as much or more receivers than senders of the gospel.

Also, we may need to rework our *teaching/learning* approach to missions. Although our American egos are at stake again, we may find that the young and the poor of the Two-Thirds World have as much or more to teach us than we have to teach them. Any American at Lausanne II learned the meaning of reversed teaching/learning roles with Christians of the Two-Thirds World. One person told of being imprisoned for his faith and condemned to clean sewers while stand-ing knee-deep in human waste. Yet, in the sewer he began to sing "I Come to the Garden Alone":

And He walks with me,

And He talks with me,

And He tells me I am His own,

And the voice I hear,

Falling on my ear,

None other has ever known.

His singing in the cesspool so convicted his captors that they became Christians and released him to win his whole village for Christ. His lesson is one that we cannot teach, but one that we must learn.

How then do we as American Christians serve as missionaries in a worldwide awakening? Our affluence, our education, our history and our color all work against us. Must we reject who and what we are? With vigor, I reject the notion that we should play the games of denying our identity as affluent Americans or resorting to the pre-tense of poverty. Instead I raise the question "Can we turn the tables on our *leading/serving* motive for missions?" This is the incarnational question Jesus himself answered when he said, "Whoever wants to become great among you must be your servant, and whoever wants to be first must be slave of all" (Mk 10:43-44). There is no substitute for the spirit of servanthood. The young and poor of the earth, wheth-er at home or abroad, know immediately whether or not we perceive ourselves as leaders or servants.

Henri Nouwen, in his book *In the Name of Jesus,* gives us an image of our posture in the worldwide awakening. When Jesus recommis-sioned Peter for servant-leadership after the resurrection and foretold the death by which Peter would die, Nouwen says that he used the image of "outstretched arms in total trust, even if it means downward mobility to a cross."[3] This is the image of the Incarnation and the attitude of servanthood which crosses the barriers between the di-verse worlds of rich and poor, young and old, learned and unlearned, North and South, East and West.

Not long ago I participated in my first foot-washing service. Stripping off the proud colors of my academic hood, the prerogatives of my presidential robe and the pious vestments of my clerical status, I took a towel, wrapped it around my waist, knelt on the floor and poured water in a basin. Sliding the bowl ahead of me, I moved on my knees to wash the feet of people who represented different roles, status and segments of our campus community. Slipping off a shoe at a time, I washed and dried:

☐ a narrow, yellow-skinned foot that characterized an Asian ancestry,

☐ a perspiring foot that betrayed discomfort in a public setting,

☐ an alabaster foot so dainty that it snuggled neatly into the palm of my hand,

☐ an outsized foot so big that I almost chuckled as it overran the borders of the bowl,

☐ a trembling foot of a prominent scholar that caught me completely by surprise,

☐ a heavily veined foot that showed the sign of advancing age.

In those feet I saw the whole world come together. I knelt before a microcosm of the world, its people and their needs—without regard to race, sex, age or status, including the brilliant and the troubled, the old and the young, the clumsy and the dainty, the calm and the anxious, the secure and the fearful. I knew all of the people face-to-face as their president, but until that moment I didn't know them hand-to-foot as their servant. The lesson will never be forgotten: *When we kneel as servants at the foot of the cross, the whole world comes together.*

Epilog:

Postscript to a College Student

We have come full circle. From the prayer of passion and the sense of urgency with which we began, our insights into the Great Awakenings of the past led us to a spiritual imperative.

. . . If there is an air of expectation for religious revival in the 1990s; . . . if the stirrings of the Spirit are evident among us; . . . if God again begins a Great Awakening with Christian students on the college campus; . . . if the Great Awakening of the 1990s is worldwide—*we know what we must do.*

Our spiritual imperative is to ask the question, *Am I ready, willing and open to the outpouring of God's Spirit if he should begin with me?*

We leave this book unfinished, not as a poem that is abandoned in despair, but as a prayer that is left open with hope. If you are ready, willing and open to the movement of the Spirit in the 1990s, you will write the next chapter in the coming Great Awakening.

Notes

Chapter 1: Stirrings of the Spirit

[1]John Naisbitt and Patricia Aburdene, *Megatrends 2000* (New York: William Morrow, 1990).

[2]Anthony F. C. Wallace, "Revitalization Movements: Some Theoretical Considerations for their Comparative Study," *American Anthropology* 58 (1956): 264-81.

[3]Jean-Paul Sartre, *Being and Nothingness*, trans. Hazel E. Barnes (London: Methuen, 1957), p. 566.

[4]Thomas A. Harris, *I'm O.K., You're O.K.: A Practical Guide to Transactional Analysis* (New York: Harper & Row, 1969).

[5]Keith Miller, *The Taste of New Wine* (Waco, Tex.: Word Books, 1965).

[6]Robert E. Coleman, ed., *One Divine Moment* (Old Tappan, N. J.: Fleming H. Revell, 1970).

[7]Herman Kahn and Anthony J. Weiner, *The Year 2000* (New York: Macmillan, 1967).

[8]Alexander W. Astin and Calvin B. T. Lee, *The Invisible Colleges: A Profile of Small Private Colleges with Limited Resources* (New York: McGraw Hill, 1972).

[9]Kenneth Kantzer, "Decadence, American Style," *Christianity Today*, August 7, 1987, p. 12.

[10]Carl F. H. Henry, *Twilight of a Great Civilization: The Drift toward Neo-Paganism* (Westchester, Ill.: Crossway Books, 1988).

[11]Charles Colson, *Against the Night: Living in the New Dark Ages* (Ann Arbor, Mich.: Servant Publications, 1989).

[12]William Muehl, "The Myth of Self-Evident Truths," *The Christian Century*, November 2, 1977, p. 1000.

[13]Robert N. Bellah, et al., *Habits of the Heart: Individualism and Commitment in American Life* (Berkeley, Calif.: University of California, 1986).

[14]Studs Terkel, *The Great Divide: Second Thoughts on the American Dream*

(New York: Pantheon Books, 1988).
[15]Richard Neuhaus, *The Naked Public Square* (Grand Rapids, Mich.: Eerdmans, 1986).
[16]Robert Wuthnow, *The Struggle for America's Soul* (Grand Rapids, Mich.: Eerdmans, 1989).

Chapter 2: Heirs of a Haystack
[1]Keith J. Hardman, "Did You Know?" *Christian History* 3:3 (issue 23): 4.
[2]Robert N. Bellah, et al., *Habits of the Heart* (New York: Harper & Row, 1985), p. 28
[3]John A. Brubacher and Willis Rudy, *Higher Education in Transition: A History of American Colleges and Universities, 1636-1976,* 3rd edition (New York: Harper & Row, 1976), p. 41.
[4]Nathan Hatch, *The Democratization of American Christianity* (New Haven, Conn.: Yale University Press, 1989), p. 57.
[5]Keith J. Hardman, "The Time for Prayer: The Third Great Awakening," *Christian History* 3:3 (issue 23): 33.
[6]William G. McLoughlin, *Revivals, Awakenings, and Reform* (Chicago: The University of Chicago Press, 1978), p. 141.
[7]Gilbert H. Barnes, quoted in Keith J. Hardman, "In the Wake of the Second Great Awakening," *Christian History* 3:3 (issue 23): 31.
[8]Brubacher and Rudy, *Higher Education in Transition,* p. 71.
[9]McLoughlin, *Revivals,* p. 178.
[10]David M. Howard, *Student Power in World Evangelism* (Downers Grove, Ill.: InterVarsity Press, 1970), p. 87.
[11]Timothy L. Smith, *Revivalism and Social Reform* (New York: Abingdon Press, 1957), pp. 148-77.
[11]Ibid.

Chapter 3: The Cycle of the Spirit
[1]J. Edwin Orr, *Evangelical Awakenings in Africa* (Minneapolis: Bethany Fellowship, 1975), p. vii.
[2]J. Edwin Orr, *Campus Aflame* (Glendale, Calif.: Regal Books, 1971), p. 237.
[3]Anthony F. C. Wallace, "Revitalization Movements: Some Theoretical Considerations for their Comparative Study," *American Anthropology* 58 (1956): 264-65.
[4]Richard Lovelace, *Dynamics of Spiritual Life: An Evangelical Theology of Renewal* (Downers Grove, Ill.: InterVarsity Press, 1979), p. 79.
[5]Quoted in William G. McLoughlin, *Revivals, Awakenings, and Reform* (Chicago: The University of Chicago Press, 1978), p. 172.
[6]Howard Snyder, *Signs of the Spirit* (Grand Rapids, Mich.: Zondervan, 1989), pp. 61-62.
[7]Ibid., p. 292.

[8]Robert E. Coleman, ed., *One Divine Moment* (Old Tappan, N. J.: Fleming H. Revell, 1970), p. 107.

Chapter 4: The Campus: Center of Stress

[1]Christopher Lasch, *The Culture of Narcissism* (New York: W. W. Norton, 1978).

[2]Robert Ringer, *Looking Out for Number One* (New York: Funk & Wagnalls, 1977).

[3]Daniel Yankelovich, *New Rules: Living in a World Turned Upside Down* (New York: Random House, 1981), pp. 4-5.

[4]Ibid., p. 8.

[5]Ibid., p. 10.

[6]Robert N. Bellah, et al., *Habits of the Heart: Individualism and Commitment in American Life* (Berkeley, Calif.: University of California, 1986), p. 47.

[7]Ibid., pp. 41ff.

[8]Reported in *The Chronicle of Higher Education*, January 24, 1990, p. A32.

[9]Frank Newman, *Higher Education and American Resurgence* (Princeton, N.J.: Carnegie Foundation for the Advancement of Teaching, 1985), p. xiv.

[10]Allan Bloom, *The Closing of the American Mind: Education and the Crisis of Reason* (New York: Simon and Schuster, 1987), p. 25.

[11]James Davison Hunter, *Evangelicalism: The Coming Generation* (Chicago: The University of Chicago Press, 1987), pp. 73-74.

[12]Ibid., p. 213.

[13]C. Robert Pace, *Education and Evangelism: A Profile of Protestant Colleges* (New York: McGraw-Hill, 1972), p. 107.

Chapter 5: The Student: Candidate for Conversion

[1]Karl Menninger, *Whatever Became of Sin?* (New York: Hawthorn Books, 1973).

[2]M. Scott Peck, *People of the Lie: The Hope for Healing Human Evil* (New York: Simon & Schuster, 1983).

[3]F. Scott Peck, *The Road Less Traveled* (New York: Simon & Schuster, 1978).

[4]Charles A. Reich, *The Greening of America* (New York: Bantam Books, 1971), p. 429.

[5]Robert E. Coleman, ed., *One Divine Moment* (Old Tappan, N. J.: Fleming H. Revell, 1970), p. 75.

[6]Vernon Grounds, *Radical Commitment* (Portland, Ore.: Multnomah Press, 1984), pp. 37-46.

Chapter 6: The Cell: School for Spirituality

[1]David M. Howard, *Student Power in World Evangelism* (Downers Grove, Ill.: InterVarsity Press, 1970), p. 68.

[2]C. Howard Hopkins, *History of the Y.M.C.A. in North America* (New York:

Association Press, 1951).

[3]Ibid., p. 298.

[4]C. E. Vulliamy, *John Wesley* (London: Geoffrey Bles, 1931), p. 60, quoted in Howard Snyder, *Signs of the Spirit* (Grand Rapids, Mich.: Zondervan, 1989), pp. 194-95.

[5]Ibid., p. 197.

[6]Henri Nouwen, *In the Name of Jesus: Reflections on the Future of Christian Leadership* (New York: Crossroads, 1989), p. 38.

[7]Elton Trueblood, *The New Man for Our Time* (New York: Harper & Row, 1970), p. 79.

[8]Snyder, *Signs of the Spirit,* p. 35.

[9]Lyle Schaller, *Assimilating New Members* (Nashville: Abingdon Press, 1978), p. 111.

[10]Snyder, *Signs of the Spirit,* p. 293.

Chapter 7: The Network. Instrument for Evangelism

[1]Richard Paul Heitzenrater, "John Wesley and the Oxford Methodists," (Ph.D. diss., Duke University, 1972), pp. 229, 232.

[2]William Warren Sweet, quoted in Keith J. Hardman, "Seasons of the Spirit," *Christian History* 3:3 (issue 23): 6.

[3]C. Robert Pace, *Education and Evangelism: A Profile of Protestant Colleges* (New York: McGraw-Hill, 1972), p. 9.

[4]John Naisbitt, *Megatrends* (New York: Warner Books, 1982), pp. 1-2.

Chapter 8: The Leader: Agent of Hope

[1]Nathan Hatch, *The Democratization of American Christianity* (New Haven, Conn.: Yale University Press, 1989), p. 4.

[2]Mrs. Howard Taylor, *Borden of Yale* (Chicago: Moody Press, n.d.), p. 235.

[3]George Gallup, Jr., and Jim Castelli, *The People's Religion* (New York: Macmillan, 1989), pp. 253-55.

[4]Hatch, *Democratization of American Christianity,* p. 86.

[5]Ibid., p. 4.

[6]Ibid., pp. 217-19.

Chapter 9: The Church: Body for Renewal

[1]Studs Terkel, *The Great Divide: Second Thoughts on the American Dream* (New York: Pantheon Books, 1988).

[2]George Gallup, Jr., and Jim Castelli, *The People's Religion* (New York: Macmillan, 1989), p. 90.

[3]Ibid.

[4]Ibid., p. 21.

[5]Greeley, *Religious Change in America* (Cambridge, Mass.: Harvard University Press), pp. 32ff.

[6]John Naisbitt and Patricia Aburdene, *Megatrends 2000* (New York: William Morrow, 1990), pp. 277-84.
[7]Gallup, *People's Religion*, p. 265.
[8]William A. Henry III, "Beyond the Melting Pot," *Time,* April 9, 1990, p. 28.

Chapter 10: The Culture: Field for Reform

[1]Edwin S. Gaustad, *Faith of our Fathers: Religion and the New Nation* (San Francisco: Harper & Row, 1987), p. 113.
[2]Ibid., p. 139.
[3]John Naisbitt and Patricia Aburdene, *Megatrends 2000* (New York: William Morrow, 1990), p. 13.
[4]Hans Küng, *Theology for the Third Millennium* (New York: Doubleday, 1988), p. 175.
[5]Ibid., p. 206.
[6]John R. W. Stott, ed., *The Year 2000* (Downers Grove, Ill.: InterVarsity Press, 1983).
[7]George Gallup, Jr., *Forecast 2000* (New York: William Morrow, 1984), pp. 12-13.
[8]Küng, *Third Millennium*, pp. 255-56.
[9]Naisbitt and Aburdene, *Megatrends 2000,* p. 16.
[10]Elton Trueblood, *The New Man for Our Time* (New York: Harper & Row, 1970), p. 126.
[11]Charles H. Malik, *The Two Tasks* (Westchester, Ill.: Cornerstone Books, 1980), p. 34.
[12]Nathan Hatch, *The Democratization of American Christianity* (New Haven, Conn.: Yale University Press, 1989), p. 219.

Chapter 11: Anticipating the Great Awakening

[1]Nathan Hatch, *The Democratization of American Christianity* (New Haven, Conn.: Yale University Press, 1989), p. 5.
[2]Samuel Wilson and John Siewert, eds., *Mission Handbook: North American Protestant Ministries Overseas,* 13th edition (Monrovia, Calif.: Missions Advanced Research and Communications Center, 1986), p. 43.
[3]Henri Nouwen, *In the Name of Jesus: Reflections on the Future of Christian Leadership* (New York: Crossroads, 1989), p. 62.

Bibliography

Abraham, William J. *The Coming Great Revival: Recovering the Full Evangelical Tradition.* San Francisco: Harper & Row, 1984.

Astin, Alexander W., and Calvin B. T. Lee. *The Invisible Colleges: A Profile of Small Private Colleges with Limited Resources.* Eighth of a series of profiles sponsored by the Carnegie Commission on Higher Education. New York: McGraw Hill, 1972.

Bellah, Robert N., et al. *Habits of the Heart: Individualism and Commitment in American Life.* New York: Harper & Row, 1985.

Bloom, Allan. *The Closing of the American Mind: Education and the Crisis of Reason.* New York: Simon and Schuster, 1987.

Coleman, Robert E., ed. *One Divine Moment.* Old Tappan, N.J.: Fleming H. Revell, 1970.

Colson, Charles. *Against the Night: Living in the New Dark Ages.* Ann Arbor, Mich.: Servant Publications, 1989.

De Pree, Max. *Leadership Is an Art.* East Lansing, Mich.: Michigan State University Press, 1988.

de Tocqueville, Alexis. *Democracy in America.* Trans. by Henry Reeve. 2 vols. New York: Schocken Books, 1961.

Eels, Robert, and Bartell Nyberg. *The Lonely Walk: The Life of Senator Mark Hatfield.* Portland, Ore.: Multnomah Press, 1979.

Gallup, George, Jr., and Jim Castelli. *The People's Religion.* New York: Macmillan, 1989.

Gaustad, Edwin S. *Faith of Our Fathers: Religion and the New Nation.* San Francisco: Harper & Row, 1987.

Greeley, Andrew M. *Religious Change in America.* Cambridge, Mass.:

Harvard University Press, 1989.

Grounds, Vernon. *Radical Commitment.* Portland, Ore.: Multnomah Press, 1984.

Harris, Thomas A. *I'm OK, You're OK: A Practical Guide to Transactional Analysis.* New York: Harper & Row, 1969.

Hatch, Nathan O. *The Democratization of American Christianity.* New Haven, Conn.: Yale University Press, 1989.

Henry, Carl F. H. *Twilight of a Great Civilization: the Drift Toward Neo-Paganism.* Westchester, Ill.: Crossway Books, 1988.

Hopkins, C. Howard. *History of the Y.M.C.A. in North America.* New York: Association Press, 1951.

Howard, David M. *Student Power in World Evangelism.* Downers Grove, Ill.: InterVarsity Press, 1970.

Hunter, James Davison. *Evangelicalism: The Coming Generation.* Chicago: The University of Chicago Press, 1987.

Küng, Hans. *Theology for the Third Millennium.* New York: Doubleday, 1988.

Lasch, Christopher. *The Culture of Narcissism.* New York: W. Norton & Company, 1978.

Lindsey, Hal. *The Road to Holocaust.* New York: Bantam Books, 1989.

Lovelace, Richard. *Dynamics of Spiritual Life: An Evangelical Theology of Renewal.* Downers Grove, Ill.: InterVarsity Press, 1979.

McLoughlin, William G. *Modern Revivalism.* New York: The Ronald Press Company, 1959.

——————. *Revivals, Awakenings, and Reform.* Chicago: The University of Chicago Press, 1978.

Mains, David R. *The Sense of His Presence.* Waco, Tex.: Word Books, 1988.

Malik, Charles H. *The Two Tasks.* Westchester, Ill.: Cornerstone Books, 1980.

Menninger, Karl. *Whatever Became of Sin?* New York: Hawthorn Books, 1973.

Miller, Keith. *The Taste of New Wine.* Waco, Tex.: Word Books, 1965.

Mott, John R. *The Evangelization of the World in This Generation.*

New York: Student Volunteer Movement for Foreign Missions, 1901.

Naisbitt, John. *Megatrends.* New York: Warner Books, 1982.

Naisbitt, John, and Patricia Aburdene. *Megatrends 2000.* New York: William Morrow and Company, Inc., 1990.

Neuhaus, Richard. *The Naked Public Square.* Grand Rapids, Mich.: Eerdmans, 1986.

Newman, Frank. *Higher Education and American Resurgence.* Princeton, N.J.: Carnegie Foundation for the Advancement of Teaching, 1985.

Nouwen, Henri J. M. *In the Name of Jesus: Reflections on the Future of Christian Leadership.* New York: Crossroads, 1989.

Orr, J. Edwin. *Campus Aflame.* Glendale, Calif.: Regal Books, 1971.

——————. *The Second Evangelical Awakening.* London: Marshall, Morgan & Scott, 1949.

——————. *Good News in Bad Times.* Grand Rapids, Mich.: Zondervan, 1953.

Pace, C. Robert. *Education and Evangelism: A Profile of Protestant Colleges.* Eleventh in a series of profiles sponsored by the Carnegie Commission on Higher Education. New York: McGraw-Hill, 1972.

Peck, M. Scott. *People of the Lie: The Hope for Healing Human Evil.* New York: Simon & Schuster, 1983.

Peretti, Frank. *Piercing the Darkness.* Westchester, Ill.: Crossway Books, 1989.

——————. *This Present Darkness.* Westchester, Ill.: Crossway Books, 1986.

Reich, Charles A. *The Greening of America.* New York: Random House, 1970.

Ringer, Robert. *Looking Out for Number One.* New York: Funk & Wagnalls, 1977.

Smith, Timothy L. *Revivalism and Social Reform.* New York: Abingdon Press, 1957.

Snyder, Howard A. *Signs of the Spirit.* Grand Rapids, Mich.: Academie Books, 1989.

"Spiritual Awakenings in North America." *Christian History.* Volume 8, no. 3, issue 23.

Stott, John R. W., ed. *The Year 2000.* Downers Grove, Ill.: InterVarsity Press, 1983.

_____ . *Your Mind Matters.* Downers Grove, Ill.: InterVarsity Press, 1973.

Terkel, Studs. *The Great Divide: Second Thoughts on the American Dream.* New York: Pantheon Books, 1988.

Vaux, Kenneth. *Birth Ethics: Religious and Cultural Values in the Genesis of Life.* New York: The Crossroad Publishing Company, 1989.

Wuthnow, Robert. *The Struggle for America's Soul.* Grand Rapids, Mich.: William B. Eerdmans Publishing Company, 1989.

Yankelovich, Daniel. *New Rules: Living in a World Turned Upside Down.* New York: Random House, 1981.